World History
SIMULATIONS

Written by Max W. Fischer

Illustrated by Cheryl Buhler

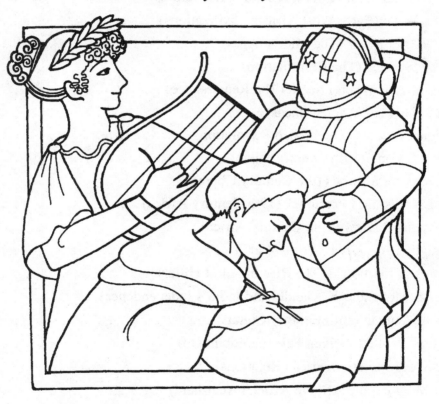

Teacher Created Materials, Inc.
P.O. Box 1040
Huntington Beach, CA 92647
©1993 Teacher Created Materials, Inc.
Made in U.S.A.

Teacher Created Materials

ISBN 1-55734-481-7

Table of Contents

Introduction

History would be so fascinating if one could only relive it.

In technology's never-ending march, man's innovations may someday perpetuate time travel by which students might learn directly from the past. Until such a time, innovative techniques such as simulations will serve to bring the events of the past into the present.

The ninety-six pages of *World History Simulations* are filled with activities designed to involve students affectively in order that they may gain ownership over the concepts presented about our world's past. Simulations, problem-solving dilemmas, and review game simulations excite students to want to learn about the causes and implications of world events as they often changed the course of history and as they affect us today.

Many of the simulations in this unit place students in the middle of a situation relevant to a famous episode in history. Students do get involved! The activities may be used as anticipatory sets for an upcoming lesson or unit. Some simulation activities can be used to bring closure to a lesson already covered. Encompassing cooperative learning, many of the activities stress critical thinking skills and/or cognitive review of test-based material.

World History Simulations has been developed to supplement whatever world history test or curriculum guide the classroom teacher may be utilizing. Most of the activities can be completed within a thirty minute time frame. A few are organized to specifically accompany an entire period of world history. This instructional aid easily accompanies the teacher and students through the history text as it follows a chronological order of scenarios. Furthermore, each activity is structured in an easy-to-follow lesson plan format that teachers will appreciate.

Success with Simulations

The activities in *World History Simulations* have been selected in order to get students involved with history by actually simulating conditions of a particular historical era within the limited confines of the school environment.

Whether you intend to use a simulation for the purposes of introduction, review, or as part of the closure process, establish procedures throughout each unit that will maintain consistency and organization. Suggestions on how to best utilize and store the units in this book follow.

Simulation Format

Each simulation begins with a lesson plan designed to assist the teacher with the preparations and procedures necessary and closes with valuable background information which connects the simulation to the historical events being studied. The lesson plan for each simulation follows this format:

- Title of Simulation
- Topic
- Objective
- Materials
- Preparation
- Procedure
- For Discussion (where applicable)
- Background
- Follow-Up (where applicable)

Storing Simulations

As you use each activity, you will want to save the components of the simulation by using a readily available and well organized system which will serve the future as well as the present. Labeled file folders or large manila envelopes can be easily sorted and organized by simulation units and kept in a file box. Pages that will be duplicated or made into overhead transparencies can be easily stored in the file folders or envelopes. Game cards, labels, etc., should be placed in envelopes or resealable plastic bags before storing them in their respective folders. If possible, use index paper or heavy stock for reproduced items, such as game pieces, that will be used over and over again. Laminating will help preserve these items.

Outside materials such as candy or plastic spoons should be readily available and noted on the outside of the activity's folder to serve as a reminder that these items need to be accessible for the simulation.

Once the simulations have been organized into a file box, you will be prepared for each unit on a moment's notice.

Let the simulations begin!

Cooperative Learning Teams

Cooperative learning is an important instructional strategy because it can be used as an integral part of many educational processes. It is made-to-order for thinking activities. The cooperative learning process acts as a powerful motivational tool.

Many of the activities in this unit involve the cooperative learning process in a team effort to find solutions or come to conclusions regarding the simulations. With this in mind, consider the following four basic components of cooperative learning as you initiate cooperative team activities.

1. **In cooperative learning all group members need to work together to accomplish the task.** No one is finished until the whole group is finished and/or has come to consensus. The task or activity needs to be designed so that members are not each completing their own part but are working to complete one product together.

2. **Cooperative learning groups should be heterogeneous.** It is helpful to start by organizing groups so that there is a balance of abilities within and between groups. Some of the simulations in this book, however, require a specific type of grouping for cooperative teams in order to achieve the simulation objective. Under such circumstances, a balanced, heterogeneous, cooperative learning team arrangement will not be appropriate for the success of the simulation.

3. **Cooperative learning activities need to be designed so that each student contributes** to the group, and individual group members can be assessed on their performance. This can be accomplished by assigning each member a role that is essential to the completion of the task or activity. When input must be gathered from all members of the group, no one can go along for a free ride.

4. **Cooperative learning teams need to know the social as well as the academic objectives** of a lesson. Students need to know what they are expected to learn and how they are supposed to be working together to accomplish the learning. Students need to process or think and talk about how they worked on social skills as well as to evaluate how well their group worked on accomplishing the academic objective. Social skills are not something that students automatically know; these skills need to be taught.

Rebus Treasure

Topic

Ancient civilizations that left behind a form of written language

Objective

Students will solve a rebus puzzle in order to find the hidden "treasure."

Materials

- pages 8 and 9, reproduced (one copy of teacher's choice for each student)
- a teacher selected treasure that will serve as an incentive for the students (e.g., pack of sugarless gum, pieces of fruit, pencils, erasers, etc.). There should be an adequate amount to share among the members of the largest student learning team. (See page 94 for other incentive ideas.)

Preparation

1. Make copies of one of the rebuses on pages 8 and 9 or create one tailored for your classroom.

2. Obtain the student incentive.

Procedure

1. Divide the class into cooperative learning teams.

2. Choose a rebus based on where you intend to hide the incentive. One of the prepared rebuses on pages 8 and 9 may be used if the class environment is conducive to its solution. If not, prepare one of original design to fit classroom needs.

3. Provide each student with a copy of the rebus. Groups should be given a specific time limit to decipher the puzzle, usually no more than five minutes.

6

Rebus Treasure *(cont.)*

Procedure *(cont.)*

4. Since it is possible that more than one group could solve the rebus in the time allotted, plan a rational method for choosing a team for the initial search attempt. A random draw of team names from a hat could be one method used to break a tie. A less arbitrary measure would be to allow the first opportunity to solve the rebus to the team that most closely follows a specified set of directions and has completed the solution.

   An alternative would be to move around the classroom garnering the responses from each team within the specified time allotment. In this situation, the first team to whisper the correct answer to the puzzle would subsequently gain access to the treasure hunt. The teacher should note successive completion times of the other teams should that become necessary in procedure 5.

5. The selected learning group will then have a short period of time (about one minute) to locate the prize. If the group cannot find the treasure within the minute, the second ranked team would be afforded a sixty-second quest. This rotation would be followed until either the prize was found or every team was given an opportunity to look.

Background

"Rebus Treasure" is simply an anticipatory set designed to lead into the discussion of ancient written languages whether from Neanderthal pictographs or Egyptian hieroglyphics. It can be completed in about ten minutes time with little set-up required. However, it does an effective job of focusing students on the idea that early civilizations often utilized concrete images for symbols representing sounds and/or ideas.

Follow-Up

Encourage students to create their own symbolic alphabet employing various geometric or pictographic designs.

Names _____

Reveal the Rebus

How quickly can you solve this rebus? Your teacher will provide you with the rules and time limit in which to find the solution. Write your solution at the bottom of the page.

Solution:

_____

- -

Note to the teacher: Fold this page under (along the dashed line) before reproducing.

Solution: Look in the cardboard box.

Reveal the Rebus

How quickly can you solve this rebus? Your teacher will provide you with the rules and time limit in which to find the solution. Write your solution at the bottom of the page.

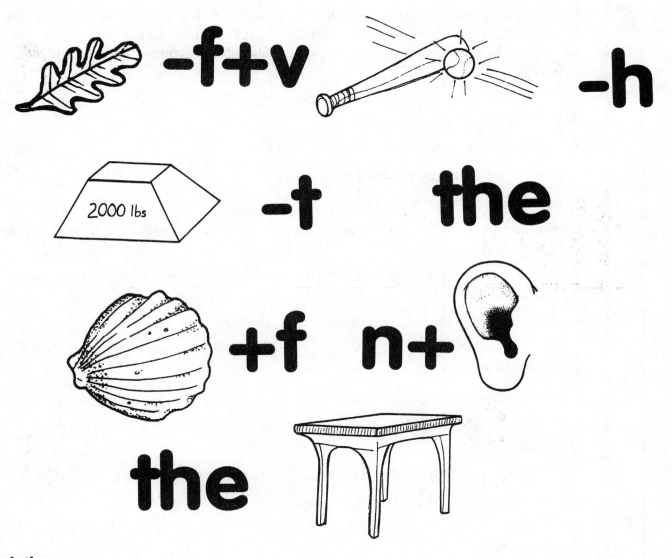

Solution:

_____

_____

- -

Note to the teacher: Fold this page under (along the dashed line) before reproducing.

Solution: Leave it on the shelf near the table.

Conquest

Topic

Ancient civilizations of the Middle East

Objective

Students will review pertinent information from their unit(s) on civilizations of the Middle East and Near East. They will utilize latitude-longitude coordinates to locate specific places on a map. They will judge geographic spatial relationships in comparing two maps of the same region.

Materials

- one overhead transparency of pages 14 and 15
- page 14, reproduced (one copy per student)
- an overhead projector with marker
- one reproduced set of eight "Ancient Cities" cards reproduced on heavy stock or index paper (page 13)
- one set of teacher-prepared review questions to be used in preparation for an upcoming chapter or unit test
- pages 16 and 17, reproduced as needed for Follow-Up (page 12)

Preparation

1. Reproduce the gridded map of the Middle East on page 14 for each student.
2. Make overhead transparencies of pages 14 and 15. Obtain and ready an overhead projector.
3. Reproduce and cut out the "Ancient Cities" cards on page 13 .
4. Prepare the review questions to be used.

Procedure

1. Divide the class into cooperative learning groups. Try to have five or six groups with eight being the maximum number of teams suitable for this activity.
2. Randomly distribute one of the "Ancient Cities" cards to each team. It is extremely important that each team's identity remain a secret! Not knowing the other groups' cities creates a more interesting strategy in playing "Conquest."

Conquest *(cont.)*

Procedure (cont.)

3. Distribute to each student a copy of page 14 while displaying the "Centers of Ancient Civilization" map on the overhead projector.

4. Explain to the class the basic rules of and scoring procedures for "Conquest." (See pages 11 and 12.) Each team will endeavor to answer the teacher-prepared review questions on the just completed chapter of the unit.

"Conquest" Rules

• When a team answers correctly, it will attempt to capture a rival city from the ancient Middle/Near East. Captures are undertaken when a team surmises the approximate location of an opposing city by viewing the map on page 15 on the overhead projector and calling out a latitude-longitude coordinates from the grid map.

• The teacher momentarily replaces page 15 transparency on the overhead projector with the transparency of page 14 and pinpoints the exact coordinates as announced by the team.

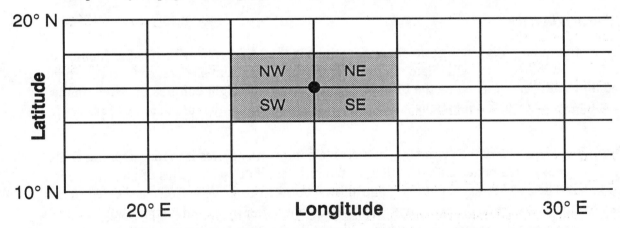

• At this point, the team must announce which of the quadrants (northeast, northwest, southeast, southwest) surrounding this point it wants to capture. In the above illustration for example, a team has called out "16 degrees north, 24 degrees east." The four quadrants around that point are all available to be taken. To do so, the teacher uses an overhead marker to initial on the page 14 transparency that square (quadrant) with the team's identifying letter (or number, or specified marker color). Previously marked squares cannot be overtaken.

• The teacher replaces the page 14 transparency with the page 15 transparency on the overhead so the class may continue to locate the cities on their copies of untitled maps while the next team gets a turn to answer a question and possibly capture a city.

• Play continues until a time or question limit has been reached, making sure each team has had an equal number of suggestions.

Conquest *(cont.)*

Procedure *(cont.)*

"Conquest" Scoring

• In order to determine a winner, all teams must first total their points from the number of correct answers they offered. The teacher may assign any point value for the correct answers.

• After point subtotals are reached, the teacher lays the page 15 transparency directly over the page 14 transparency on the overhead. This will indicate which teams are able to "conquer" or capture which cities. Any city within an occupied square is considered captured.

• Any team that captures an opposing team's city receives all of that city's points.

• When the appropriate addition and deduction of points from various teams is concluded, the team with the most points wins.

Background

The march of empires among ancient civilizations in the Middle/Near East is the foundation of this game designed to stimulate review over those very societies. Over a period of about two thousand years preceding the birth of Christ, each of the eight cultures depicted on the "Centers of Ancient Civilizations" map were at one time or another at the apex of power in this region.

This activity harnesses the students' competitive nature and applies it to map-reading skills. Students also gain a better understanding of the "rise and fall" schematics of these ancient domains. The secrecy aspect of the game allows teams to contrive various strategies. They may decide to secure their own cities first before going after opponents' strongholds. In any case, a group cannot be sure about which cities will offer the most points, and anticipation mounts until final scores are totalled.

Follow-Up

An unlabeled map of Europe is provided on page 16, accompanied by a gridded map of Europe on page 17. Teachers may adapt the European maps to another version of "Conquest" dealing with any number of topics such as the Roman Empire, the barbarian invasion of Europe, the Crusades, Napoleonic Europe, World Wars I and II. Teachers are free to delineate pertinent cities or other political entities on the unlabeled map. Preparation of materials is identical to that of the Middle East "Conquest" simulation.

Note to the teacher: Due to map projection and use of the square grid measurements on these maps, the actual latitude/longitude reading will not be totally accurate.

"Ancient Cities" Cards

See page 10 for directions.

Athens	Sparta
Memphis	Jerusalem
Nineveh	Babylon
Ur	Persepolis

Grid Map

Directions: Reproduce enough copies of this page for each student. Prepare an overhead transparency for the simulation on pages 10-12.

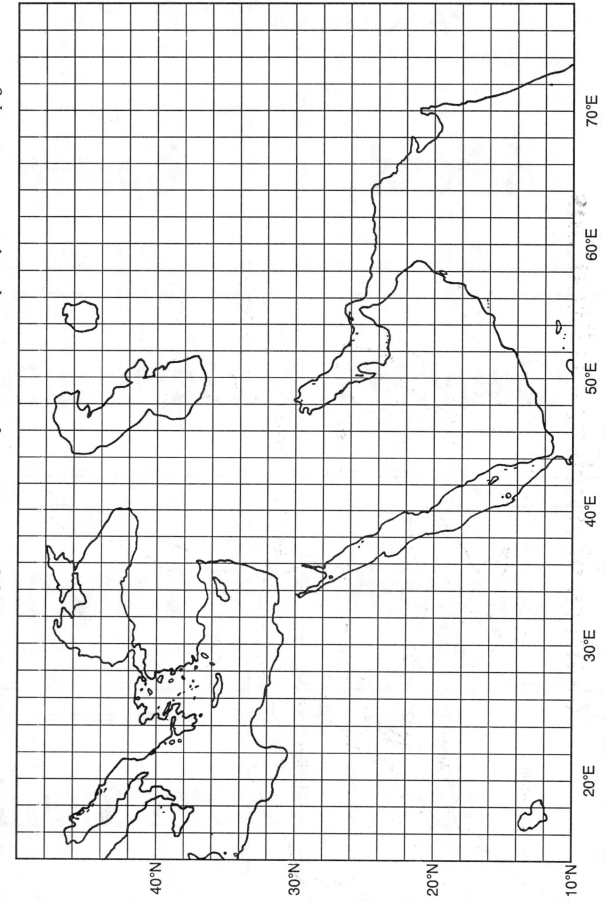

Centers of Ancient Civilizations

Directions: Prepare an overhead transparency for the simulation on pages 10-12.

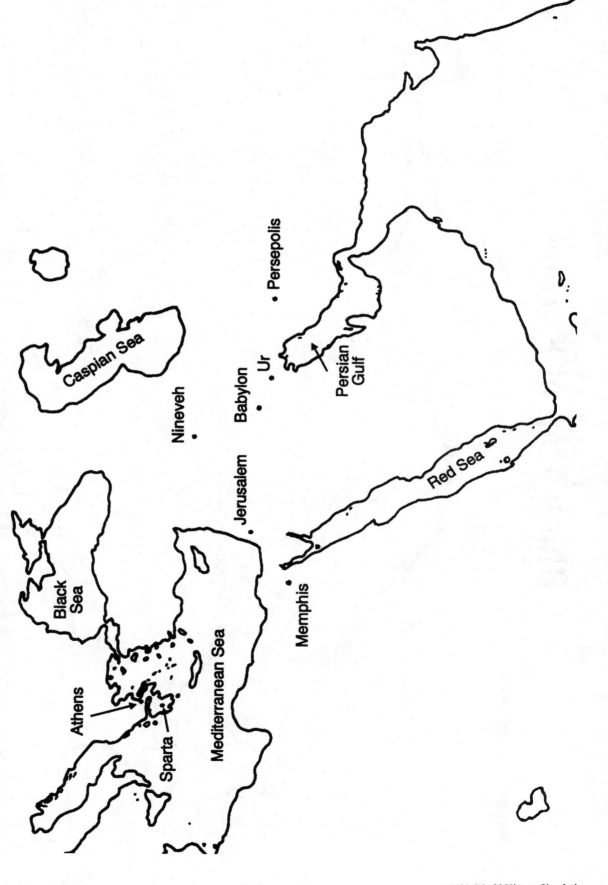

Blank Map of Europe

See page 12 for suggested uses.

16

Gridded Map of Europe

See page 12 for suggested uses.

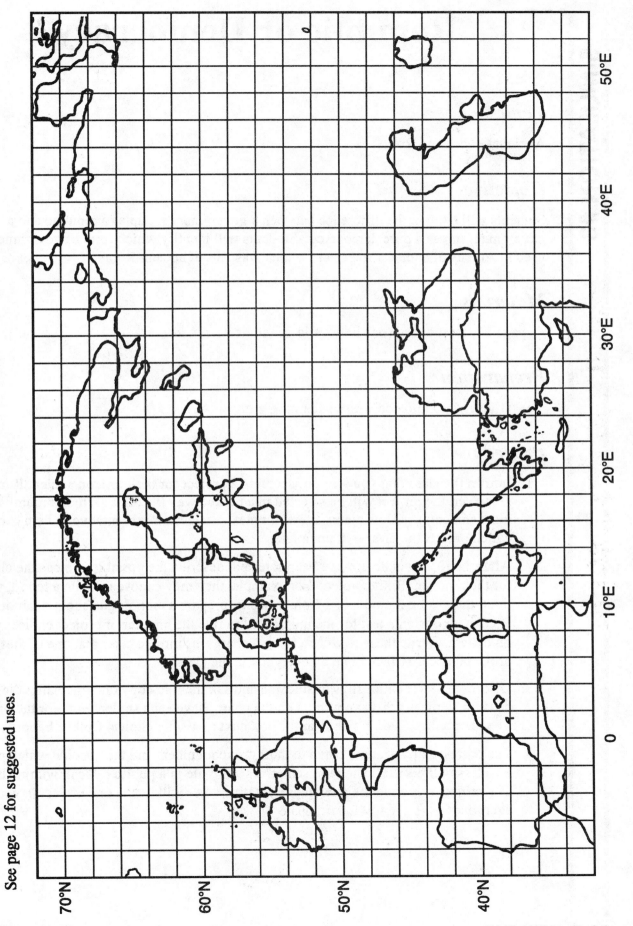

Republic or Democracy?

Topic

Ancient Greece and Rome

Objective

Students will explain the difference between a government set up as a republic and a government run as a pure democracy. Students will identify which form of government was used in Athens of ancient Greece and which was part of ancient Rome.

Materials

- page 20, reproduced (one ballot slip per student)

Preparation

1. Divide class into cooperative learning groups.

Procedure

1. Inform the class that you will be assigning a project for their unit on ancient Rome. However, the project will be selected in a unique way (i.e., in a fashion unfamiliar to most students). Allow teams a few minutes to select a representative to help choose which project the class will undertake.

2. After the representatives have been selected, describe the possible choices the class has for their ancient Rome project. For example, they may choose to write a report, make a three-dimensional model of a Roman scene, prepare a monologue about a famous Roman, or design a test for the unit. Limit to five the number of project choices you give them. Write these five choices on a chart. Inform the class that one of these project choices will be done by everyone in the class.

3. Distribute secret ballot slips to students and ask them to copy onto the ballot the five possible choices you have written on the chart. Have each student vote for the project by secret ballot, marking an X in the box next to his/her choice. Collect ballots.

4. The representatives are to listen to their group members and then decide which project the class will pursue. The representatives will vote in a public roll call within class. The project receiving the most representative votes will be the one project in which everyone in the class will participate.

Republic or Democracy? *(cont.)*

Procedure *(cont.)*

5. After the representatives have publicly cast their votes, compare the representatives' decision to the ballots cast by all individuals within the class. Ask students if they think the vote of the group's agents accurately reflects the choice of the people as exhibited by the popular vote.

6. Inform the class that the project choices most recently voted upon will actually be chosen by each individual rather than the forced selection mentioned in the simulation.

For Discussion

Discuss the following question with the class:

- Which form of choosing do you think best reflected the will of the class majority?

- Would the popular vote be the best way to make laws and run the daily business of government? Why or why not?

- Which of these forms of governing would be best for a large nation or empire?

- Which one might work well with a small population of voters?

- What was the form of government used by the people of ancient Athens in Greece? Which of the two forms we just employed did it most closely resemble?

- Why do you think the people of ancient Rome used a representative or "republic" form of government?

Background

While democracy is a legacy from the ancient Greeks, it was not a universal concept even within the city-states of Greece. Many were run by aristocratic nobility who, when they abused their power, were ousted by a tyrant who himself was a kind of vigilante nobleman. Of course, Sparta remains an example of the classic military city-state. Yet even in Athens, with its Golden Age under Pericles, the democracy that developed was only for free, male citizens whose ancestors had been citizens. Discounting women, slaves, and first generation immigrants, a veritable minority constituted the Athenian democracy.

Expansionist Rome, with numerous external threats and the need to quell the distrust of its plebeians for the ruling patricians, went to the republic form of government early in its development while its borders were still confined to the Italian peninsula. It maintained aristocratic control of the government while still allowing a voice for the average citizen.

This lesson allows the students a glimpse at how the contemporary American republic makes most of its decisions through the representative form of governance.

Secret Ballot

Reproduce and cut out the secret ballot slips below. Distribute one slip to each student. See pages 18 and 19 for directions on the use of the ballot slips.

Directions: Write the project choices on the lines below as directed by your teacher. Choose one project by placing an X in the box next to your choice. Do not sign your name to this slip.

☐ 1._____

☐ 2._____

☐ 3._____

☐ 4._____

☐ 5._____

Directions: Write the project choices on the lines below as directed by your teacher. Choose one project by placing an X in the box next to your choice. Do not sign your name to this slip.

☐ 1._____

☐ 2._____

☐ 3._____

☐ 4._____

☐ 5._____

Directions: Write the project choices on the lines below as directed by your teacher. Choose one project by placing an X in the box next to your choice. Do not sign your name to this slip.

☐ 1._____

☐ 2._____

☐ 3._____

☐ 4._____

☐ 5._____

Academic Raiders

Topic

Barbarian Germanic tribes of the fourth through ninth centuries

Objective

Students will identify three of the Germanic tribes that destroyed the western half of the Roman Empire and dominated large portions of Europe during the early Middle Ages. Over the course of several days to a week, students will create review questions from various subjects to challenge each other.

Materials

- page 24, reproduced on index paper or heavy stock (about twelve tribal chips per team)
- page 25, reproduced (Provide several copies for each team.)
- large envelopes, two per team (for storing tribal chips and question strips)

Preparation

1. Prepare tribal chips.
2. Distribute several copies of page 25 to each team. These pages will be used by each team for presenting written questions to other teams, as directed in Procedure.

Procedure

1. Divide the class into cooperative learning teams. Each team will become a tribe.
2. Have each tribe select a Germanic tribal name for itself and pass out twelve chips per tribe. Have each team write the name of the specific tribe they have chosen on each of the chips.
3. Tribe members are to prepare review questions for any academic subject matter they are currently studying with which to challenge opposing tribes (teams). While the immediate social studies curriculum may be dealing with the fall of Rome or the early Middle Ages, the questions alluded to here may be from any subject.

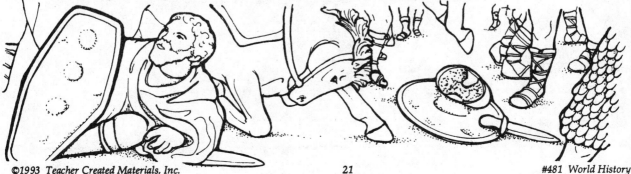

Academic Raiders *(cont.)*

Procedure *(cont.)*

4. A tribe may direct two questions to one other tribe, or it may ask a single question of any two tribes. Two questions per tribe, per day is the limit. Have each tribe write its daily questions on distributed copies of page 25.

5. Challenges to question responses can be made only during prescribed seatwork time. Have one tribe member orally request, "We'd like to challenge the _____ tribe."

6. A tribe's objective is to capture another tribe by giving its members three questions that the other team cannot correctly answer over the course of the "Academic Raiders" simulation. If a tribe fails to answer another's challenge in one minute's time, the challenged tribe loses a chip to the challenger. Any tribe that acquires three chips from another tribe captures it and rules it.

   A tribe (team) may gain more than three chips on a capture if the opposing team has one or more captures to its credit. In such an instance, the victorious tribe would garner all captured chips from that tribe in addition to the three in hand. For example, the Vandals have just secured the third chip from the Franks who have already conquered the Goths. The Vandals now lay claim to six chips altogether.

7. Questions cannot be arbitrary, vague, or misleading. They must deal with pertinent student objectives in assorted subject matter. If a question is correctly answered, no chips are gained or lost. The teacher may wish to model appropriate ways to word questions.

8. If a challenging team accuses its opponent of giving an incorrect answer when indeed the opponent's reply was correct and the challenging team's answer was wrong, the opponent secures one of the challenging team's chips.

9. Reinforcement points or awards are up to the discretion of each individual teacher. If employed, they may be given on the basis of number of chips confiscated or number of tribes subjugated.

22

Academic Raiders (cont.)

Background

The barbarian invaders from northern Europe that fell upon Rome in the fifth century were a fearsome lot. Nomadic herders who were the ancestors of the later Vikings, they resisted Roman authority and eventually overran it. They lusted for combat and over a several hundred year period controlled large sections of Europe through numerous small bands and their chieftains.

These tribes included the Vandals, Saxons, Angles, Franks, Goths, Visigoths, Ostrogoths, and Russe. They all had their roots in Scandinavia. Most spoke Germanic dialects, and as they were civilized by the vanquished masses upon whom they intruded, they became the foundation for future nations of Angles, Saxons (England and Germany), Franks (France), and Russe (Russia).

Follow-Up

Much more can be added to this activity if so desired. Students could research their particular tribe and present life style updates to the class during social studies. These updates could be in the form of oral information, artistic work, or dramatic renditions of the living conditions of these peoples. With proper bibliographic citations, such updates could earn a team a "fortification" chip by which it could fend off surrendering its third chip to any other team. Any "fortification" chip could be substituted for a regular chip and not be counted as one of the three chips that lead to capitulation.

If this competitive aspect does not appeal to you, set up a class goal whereby the objective is for the various tribes to total a specific number of combined correct answers.

Tribal Game Chips

Directions: Label, cut out, and color (if desired) each of the tribal chips for your team. Store them in an envelope.

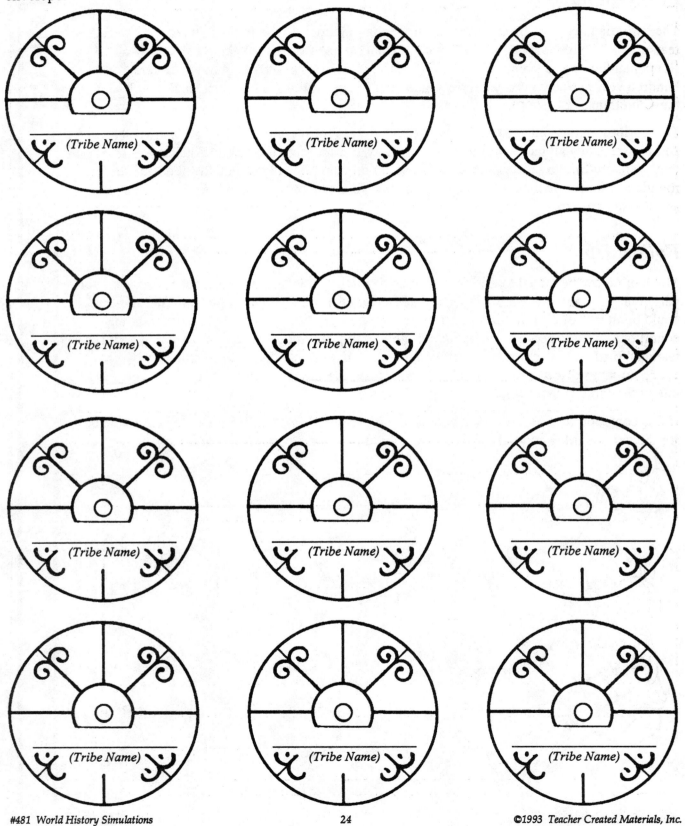

24

Tribal Queries

Directions: Cut along the dashed lines. Fill in the blanks with your daily challenge question information and distribute the questions to opposing tribes, as directed by your teacher. Store question strips in an envelope.

Our Tribe Name: _____

Date: _____

Challenge Questions:

1. _____

_____

2. _____

_____

Our Tribe Name: _____

Date: _____

Challenge Questions:

1. _____

_____

2. _____

_____

Our Tribe Name: _____

Date: _____

Challenge Questions:

1. _____

_____

2. _____

_____

Relative Merit

Topic

Early West African commerce

Objective

Students will realize the value of salt in early West African civilizations. They will define bartering.

Materials

- one bag of miniature candy bars (enough for one candy bar per student)
- one box of salt or several small salt packets one gets at a fast food restaurant
- one piece of gold costume jewelry
- one copy of Information/Request Letter (page 29) for each student
- grocery bags or plastic storage bags (one for each student)

Preparation

1. Obtain the materials listed above.

2. Reproduce and distribute copies of the letter on page 29 to students. Explain that the items they bring to class and the purpose for the upcoming activity will be explained in the letter. (See Follow-Up, page 28, for activity related to the take-home letter.) As each student submits materials for bartering, place his/her items in a sealed plastic or paper bag labeled with student's name and all items contained in the bag. Be sure to remind students that items brought in for trade are expendable. Therefore, students should only use items they do not need or use. Store all bags until you are ready for the bartering activity.

Note to the teacher: It is important to have extra items available in the classroom for bartering in case some students do not have items to trade. For the purpose of classroom management, you may wish to set a limit on the number or type of trade items allowed.

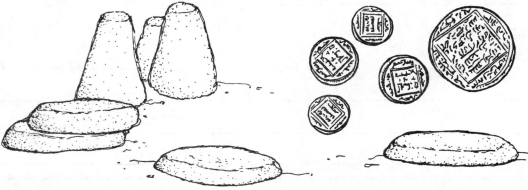

26

Relative Merit *(cont.)*

Procedure

1. Before initiating a lesson on the early West African civilizations of Ghana or Mali, distribute one miniature candy bar to each member of the class.

2. Ask the class if they (as individuals) would consider trading their candy for a packet (or even a box) of salt. The response will probably be an overwhelming "no." Ask students the following question: "Which of you would consider trading in the candy bar for the answers to tonight's homework assignment?" This question will give them cause to think. (You may actually follow through with such a trade if you are so inclined.)

3. Consider one more possible trade with the following question: "Which of you would trade the candy bar for ten additional minutes of recess?" (Again, it is the teacher's option whether or not to permit such a transaction.)

4. Hold up the salt in one hand and the gold jewelry in the other and ask, "How many of you would trade this salt for this jewelry?"

5. At this point, lead students into the upcoming lesson by saying, "Today we will be studying a time when salt was valued as much as, or even more than gold."

For Discussion

Ask the class if they have ever heard of the word "barter," and if so, what they think it means. Discuss the idea of bartering and the fact that the preceding activity in which they have been involved was designed as a way of introduction to the bartering process as it might have occurred in early civilizations. At an appropriate time, allow students to eat the miniature candy bars!

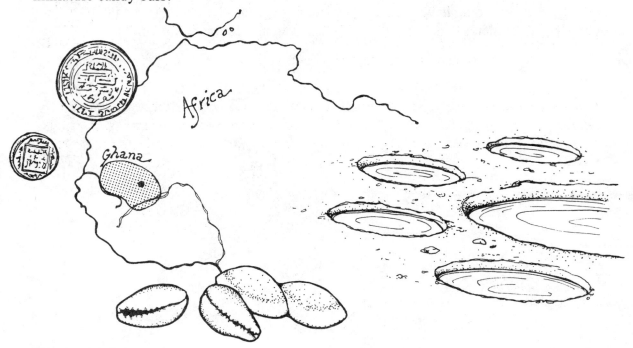

Relative Merit *(cont.)*

Background

In the early civilizations of West Africa, salt from the Sahara Desert was traded to gold-enriched areas of the sub-Saharan region. The entire commerce was the epitome of supply and demand. The desert regions had been an ocean bottom millions of years before and therefore had an abundance of salt. The quantities were so great that certain locales made dwellings out of blocks of salt. Towards the forested south, there was a dearth of salt which was prized for flavoring food and absolutely needed for sustaining life in the hot, tropical environment. There was gold however, and so each region supplied what the other valued.

Analogous to this historic commerce, the students will probably place little or no relative value on salt, given its abundance in our lives. Conversely, candy is more likely to be of value to them. When offered less work or more play time for a treat, the temptation for the possible exchange definitely rises.

Follow-Up

To this day, salt caravans traverse the same lands, and even the desert huts are still made of blocks of salt. Students may want to research the millennium-old trade and share results with the class.

Take out items students brought in for bartering. (See Preparation step 2, page 26 and Information/Request Letter, page 29.) Give each student his/her respective bag of items. Discuss the various items collected and the students' reasons for wishing to trade. Divide the class into small groups. Decide on a plan for trading among the members of each group. Will it be necessary or desirable to trade some item(s) with another group? How can this be done? After guidelines for trading have been established, have groups barter using the items brought in by the students. Discuss the activity when an agreed upon time limit has been reached.

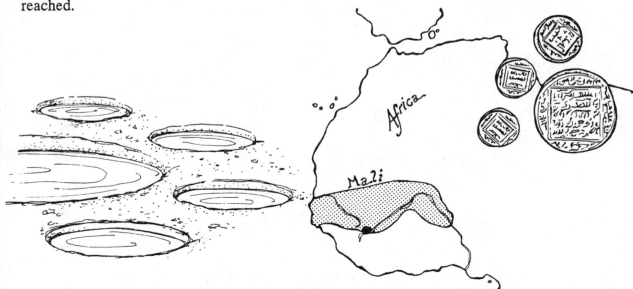

Information/Request Letter

Dear _____,

My class will be studying about early West African commerce and the barter system of trading. We will simulate bartering in class, and we need your help.

If we have any items such as used games, toys, or books that are no longer needed at home, could I bring them to school for this activity?

Please list items that I can bring to school on the lines at the bottom of this page. Then tear off the bottom portion along the dashed lines and return the bottom portion by _____.
(Date)

Thank you for donating the items.

Your _____,

_____
(Student's Signature)

- -

I, _____, will bring in the following items for bartering:
(Student's Name)

_____

_____

_____

_____

_____
(Student's Signature)

Ghana Trade

Topic

Early West African civilizations

Objective

Students will review vital teacher-created questions about early West African civilizations. They will explain how the early empire of Ghana became rich and powerful through its central geographic location.

Materials

- one set of review questions from a chapter or unit on early West African civilizations with which the teacher feels the students need to become more familiar

- a reward or reinforcer for the winning team (See page 94 for ideas.)

- Ghana Trade Name Tags (page 33) reproduced on index paper or heavy stock, colored and cut out

- Overhead transparency of Ghana Trade Score Sheet (page 34)

- Overhead projector

Preparation

1. Write original questions or locate review questions on early West African civilizations which reflect information learned in class.

2. Reproduce and cut out the Ghana Trade Name Tags.

3. Prepare the transparency of page 34 and set up an overhead projector.

30

Ghana Trade *(cont.)*

Procedure

1. Divide the class into three heterogeneous ability teams before the activity begins.

2. Explain to the class that they will be participating in a review game for an upcoming test on the early civilizations of West Africa.

3. Place the three Ghana Trade Name Tags face down on a table. Have one member from each team randomly select one of the three prepared tags. This random draw will identify each team. (Physically separate the teams within your room so that Ghana Central is placed between the other two teams.) You may wish to make a diagram for the students so that they can easily arrange themselves into their teams before the review begins.

4. The teacher then reads a question from the list he/she has designed in advance. Each question in the review game will be worth ten points.

   Saharan North is asked the first question. Whatever the team's response, it must be stated to and cleared through the Ghana Central team. If the answer is correct and Ghana Central agrees, the two teams split the ten points with five points going to each. Use the Ghana Trade Score Sheet transparency to tally points earned by each team. If the answer is incorrect and Ghana Central disagrees and gives the correct response, then Ghana Central receives all ten points for the question. Should neither team respond with the appropriate answer, no points are awarded to either team.

5. The Jungle South team is asked the second question. The same format is followed as in Procedure 4.

6. The game continues with Saharan North and Jungle South taking successive turns at answering questions while the Ghana Central team serves as the opportunist by either verifying the other team's answers or correcting them. In either case, without being asked direct questions, the Ghana Central team should keep accumulating a significant point total.

7. The game ends after a set time limit or question limit has expired.

Ghana Trade *(cont.)*

For Discussion

Students from the Saharan North and Jungle South teams will probably become annoyed over losing valuable points to Ghana Central for no apparent reason. After the game is over, be sure to ask the class if they saw any similarities between how Ghana Central obtained its points and how the empire of Ghana became rich. Ask students to compare the two situations and draw parallels (i.e., Ghana Central parallels the centrally located empire of Ghana while Saharan North and Jungle South represent the trade routes of two separated regions flowing through and controlled by the central region).

Background

The empire of Ghana was located in the savanna between the Sahara Desert to the north and the tropical rain forest along the coast of the Gulf of Guinea towards the south. It reached its zenith about a thousand years ago by controlling the trade routes that connected its adjacent regions which it separated. The salt caravans from the north and the gold traders from the south were all subject to the Ghanaian ruler's duties and other taxes for crossing his territory. While Ghana did possess fertile land, its real wealth was predicated upon its central location and the political strength of its rulers to take advantage of it.

Ghana Trade Name Tags

SAHARAN
NORTH

GHANA
CENTRAL

JUNGLE
SOUTH

Ghana Trade Score Sheet

Team ⟹	SAHARAN NORTH	GHANA CENTRAL	JUNGLE SOUTH
Tally ⟹			
Total team points ⟹			

Winner _____

Feudal M & M's®

Topic

Feudalism in medieval Europe

Objective

Students will identify the order of societal rank and loyalties within feudal Europe.

Materials

- paper cups (one for each student)

- plastic spoons or surgical latex gloves (enough for each noble and vassal)

- one 8-ounce (224 g) bag of M & M's®

- one transparency of the classroom seating diagram similar to the one on page 39

- one copy of role identification cards (page 38), reproduced on index paper, construction paper, or heavy stock

Preparation

1. Reproduce and cut out the role identification cards on page 38 in the following class percentages (approximate): Noble (10%); Vassal (30%); Peasant (55%). Prepare only one King identification card since there will be only one student in this role at any given time. For example, in a class of 21 students, roles could be assigned as follows: 1 King, 2 Nobles, 6 Vassals, and 12 Peasants. (See diagram on page 39.)

2. The Noble, Vassal, and Peasant cards need to be categorized into two respective domains: one-half of each are to be marked "A," and the other half are to be labeled with a "B." If you have a third noble, the role cards would be divided into thirds.

   Note to the teacher: Depending upon the number of students, you may have to alter the number of cards slightly to keep the approximate proportions.

   Throughout the activity there can be only one king. The ratio of total students in the class to nobles should be about 10 to 1.

3. Make a transparency of a "Feudal Classroom" that represents your students. Use the sample diagram on page 39 as a guide.

Feudal M & M's® *(cont.)*

Procedure

1. Have students draw identification role cards at random.

2. Then, depending on whether they belong to the realm of Noble A or that of Noble B, students should arrange their desks similar to the diagram on page 39, which the teacher should place on the overhead projector. (If an overhead projector is not available, simply reproduce the diagram onto a chart or copy it on the chalkboard.)

3. Arrange the room to approximate the diagram. (Availability of space will dictate the room arrangement and necessary modifications.)

4. Give each student or "member of the realm" a paper cup containing ten M & M's®. The nobles and vassals should also be given a plastic spoon or a glove. The candy is to represent the harvest reaped in a particular year by the peasants.

5. Since the peasants were paying for their protection with their crops, have the vassals confiscate six M & M's® from each peasant using their spoons or rubber gloves. (The lines on the diagram indicate the number of peasants to each vassal.)

6. From each peasant's payment, the vassal is to keep one piece and give five to his lord, the noble.

7. From each vassal's payment of fidelity, or loyalty, the noble is to keep two pieces and give three candies to the king (once again using the spoon or glove).

8. Using the classroom arrangement on page 39 and the procedures above, the final candy distribution might look like this: the peasants, 4 candies; the vassals, 12 candies; the nobles, 22 candies; the king, a lusty 46 candies.

Feudal M & M's® *(cont.)*

For Discussion

In the early medieval period, the rights of man were not a major concern; survival was. At the end of this activity, students will no doubt complain that the king now has 46 pieces of candy while they, as peasants, have but four. Turn those concerns into constructive and informative discussions about the roles within and aspects of the feudal system by asking the following questions:

- What need would the nobles and king have for all that food and material?
- What choice did the peasants have?
- Why did feudalism work?

Discuss with students the fact that meager subsistence by the peasants was preferable to being ravaged by marauding bands of outlaws and armies.

The teacher may, at an appropriate time, collect all M & M's® and distribute them equally among students. Students may also be permitted to keep their allotment of M & M's® in order to reinforce in their minds the disparity of wealth and power that existed during feudalism.

Background

"Feudal M & M's®" is a visual/kinesthetic experience to be implemented after the topic of feudalism has already been introduced. The physical make-up of the room, with the majority of M & M's® falling into the hands of a few nobles, can also help reinforce students' knowledge about an important part of the power structure of the Middle Ages. The king, while very powerful, could rarely secure power over a large area due to ambitious noblemen. By themselves, these lords were not overly threatening to a king. However, if they consolidated their strengths, they could be formidable. Note that in the class demonstration while the king had 46 pieces of candy, his two nobles totaled 44 between them. This ratio corresponds to the relative need each had to supply the infantry and knights and gives a clue to their respective numbers. There was always a sense of distrust between kings and their nobility over who controlled the kingdom. "Feudal M & M's®" reinforces the cognitive definition of feudalism.

Follow-Up

The significance of the Magna Carta lies in the defined limits of the king's power in respect to that of the nobles. It became a stabilizing factor in England's emergence out of feudalism into nationhood for that very reason. Students may research the Magna Carta as to its significance to our own American government.

Role Identification Cards

See page 35 for directions.

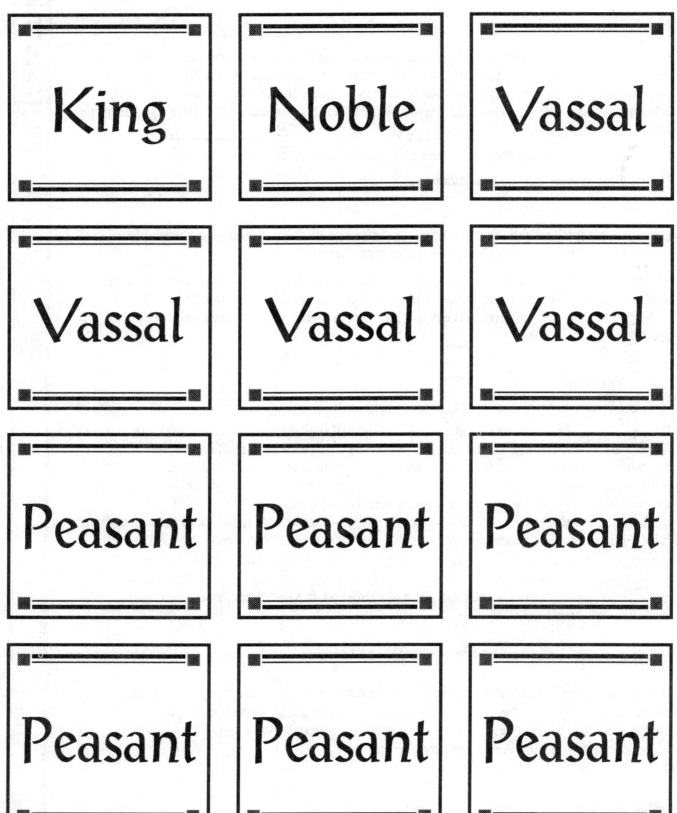

Feudal Classroom Diagram

See pages 35-37 for directions.

King

Noble A

Vassal A   Vassal A   Vassal A

Peasant A   Peasant A   Peasant A   Peasant A   Peasant A   Peasant A

Noble B

Vassal B   Vassal B   Vassal B

Peasant B   Peasant B   Peasant B   Peasant B   Peasant B   Peasant B

Sunday Service

Topic

The Reformation

Objective

Students will identify two weaknesses of the Roman Catholic Church that Martin Luther wanted to correct.

Materials

- one copy of the situation "Sunday Service" for each student

- overhead projector (optional)

Preparation

1. Reproduce copies of "Sunday Service" dilemma for each student.

Procedure:

1. Divide the class into cooperative learning teams.

2. Use this activity as a way of introducing the Reformation. Pass out copies of the dilemma, "Sunday Service." Have the class read through it silently while you read it aloud.

3. Allow the teams about three to five minutes to air the points of contention each has with the dilemma.

40

Sunday Service *(cont.)*

For Discussion

Discuss the issues that the class has raised, listing them on the chalkboard or overhead. As a transition into the lesson, let the students know that at one point in time the scenario that was just discussed was quite frequently accurate when it came to Christian worship. During the end of the Middle Ages "indulgences" were methods of buying back sins (or buying forgiveness) for yourself, your family, or even people who had passed away. Before the printing press came on the scene about 1450, most people had no access to books of any kind since they were so expensive to have hand-copied. That especially applied to the Bible, which was usually kept in Latin or Greek.

Background

Martin Luther's posting of his 95 Theses was a direct assault on the wealthiest and most powerful social institution within Europe during his day, the Roman Catholic Church. The Church with its ability to tax and crown rulers even had its own political entity, the Holy Roman Empire. In the early sixteenth century Luther's threats on the church were met with charges of heresy and an eventual death sentence.

When the Holy Roman emperor sentenced Luther to something akin to internal banishment, German nobles rallied behind Luther providing him with safe refuge. These same nobles agreed to Luther's call to end indulgences and have the Bible available in German for all the people to read and interpret for themselves. They protested these and other aspects of the Church and so became known as "protestants."

Note to the teacher: Some of your students may never have seen the inside of a church and are unaware of the difference between contemporary worship and that of five hundred years ago. However, most students will at least have an idea that something is definitely amiss in "Sunday Service."

Sunday Service Dilemma

It is Sunday morning. You are preparing to attend worship services at a local church. As you are about to enter the church, a church official greets your family with a collection plate and asks if you would like to buy some forgiveness this morning. Your parents place some money in the plate while you put in two quarters. You remember you had lied to your mother earlier in the week, and you want to buy back that indiscretion. (A quarter should do it.) You always buy a little forgiveness for dearly departed Uncle Harry who died two years ago. You figure Uncle Harry needs a lot of sins removed, so you usually buy back one or two each time you come to church.

Your family settles into a pew and prays silently. There will be another collection after the priest conducts a good part of the service in a foreign language that no one in your family understands.

The priest does finally address you in comprehendible language when he gives his hour-long sermon in which you get to hear bits and pieces of the Bible. You have heard that the Bible is the word of God, but at eight hundred dollars a copy, your family has not been able to afford one. Your parents have stated that there is no need for the expense of a Bible since the priest tells them exactly what to believe in it and interprets it for them.

As you are exiting the church, you place another quarter into the plate the church official is once again holding at the door as you leave. You really liked Uncle Harry.

Questions to Consider

What is "different" about this church? Would you want to attend it? Why or why not?

I'll Believe It When I See It

Topic

The scientific realm of the Renaissance

Objective

Students will identify one known fact of the world that was considered false and unreasonable during the early stages of the Renaissance.

Material

- page 96, reproduced (one copy per student)
- overhead transparency of page 46
- overhead projector
- pages 47 and 48, reproduced (one copy each per student)

Preparation

1. Make the overhead transparency of the graphic on page 46.

2. Prepare copies of page 47 and 48 for student inventions.

3. Prepare copies of the Brainstorming Web on page 96 for those students who need one in order to do the Follow-Up activity.

Procedure

1. Prior to a lesson on the great scientists of the early and middle Renaissance (Copernicus, Galileo, etc.), place the graphic (page 46) on an overhead projector for the students to view for four or five seconds only!

2. After removing it from the overhead projector, ask various students to state what they think the message on the transparency said. Most of the time students unanimously reply, "AKRON IN THE WINTER."

3. After students have had the opportunity to assert their views on what message was within the triangle, beg to differ with them. Openly disagree that it indeed said something different, something beyond what they saw. Be adamant and somewhat argumentative about it.

I'll Believe It When I See It *(cont.)*

Procedure *(cont.)*

4. Suggest that perhaps students could brainstorm other possible messages that were inside the triangle.

5. Allow the students a few minutes to mull over any immediate ideas. After several minutes of further haranguing, dramatically reveal the transparency again. Let it remain in view until the students catch the presence of the second "THE." (Due to the short original viewing of the phrase, the brain tends to pick out the "whole" of the message, whereas specific details take a greater time to process.)

6. Move to a formal lesson on Renaissance scientists, employing the students' recently-expressed feelings to have them understand that new ideas, no matter how much they are founded in truth, have always run the gauntlet against accepted logic.

For Discussion

Follow up with vital questioning. Ask the class how they felt while you were pressing your opinion that they were wrong about what they saw as to the actual content of the message.

Be prepared to handle replies such as "frustrated," "angry," "confused," "this teacher is very wrong," "this idea is weird." Ask students if the teacher's expressed view was causing them to hold tighter to their initial idea of what they thought they saw.

Background

When is the last time you scrutinized your spaghetti at lunch or dinner? For that matter, has any pasta ever induced more than a passing thought about its potential position on an upcoming repast? How about paper? When has plain, everyday writing paper fascinated you? When is the last time that the sun's central position in our solar system gave you a restless night's sleep?

The point to be made here is this: For hundreds of years during the Middle Ages and into the Renaissance simple items such as pasta and paper were relatively unknown to the masses in Europe.

5 lb. 1 lb. *law of falling bodies* Galileo Galilei *phases of*

44

I'll Believe It When I See It (cont.)

Background (cont.)

Scientific knowledge of the universe and its make-up was predicated upon erroneous concepts from a prior millennium. Information acquired by adventurers such as Marco Polo, and deduced by scientists such as Copernicus and Galileo was more often than not shunned and ridiculed. New ideas that went against conventional wisdom were not tolerated, let alone nurtured.

In "I'll Believe It When I See it" students are unknowingly placed into the role of purveyors of accepted logic, and the teacher plays the role of the ideological challenger. In this activity it is important for the students to realize that the same human tendencies that squelched valid ideas five hundred years ago are still with us today. Not only is it meaningful for their understanding of history, but it is also imperative in cultivating educated, contemplative citizenry of a contemporary democracy.

Follow-Up

Today new ideas and inventions are encouraged and openly accepted. Sometimes this creates a dilemma of its own. Thousands of ideas for new products or "new and improved" ideas for established products flood the market. Manufacturers are inundated with such inventions and product ideas. The dilemma becomes one of choosing the best, most efficient, least costly, and most marketable products to endorse. Have the class experience the Renaissance era in a more contemporary setting.

Select a group of students to each assume the role of purveyor of new ideas. This group will become the "Innovators." Each student will be given the task of inventing a new product that he or she will try to "sell" to the class.

The class's role is that of a manufacturing company or other institution. They could be given a title such as "Establishmentors." Use the information and activities on pages 47 and 48 to guide and encourage student "Innovators" to create a product, an invention, or a unique idea that must be "sold" to a manufacturer or institution (the class) already content with the "status quo." Have "Innovators" present the products or ideas to the "Establishmentors," who must then decide whether or not to "buy into" these new products or ideas. Discuss the points of view of both groups at the close of the activity.

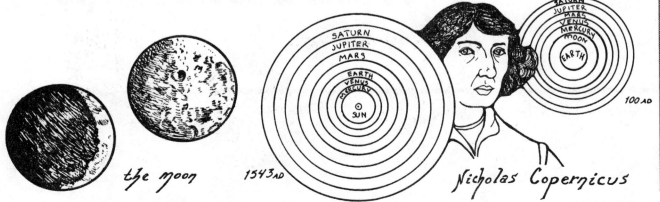

the moon   1543 AD   SATURN JUPITER MARS EARTH VENUS MERCURY SUN   SATURN JUPITER MARS VENUS MERCURY MOON EARTH 100 AD   Nicholas Copernicus

I'll Believe It When I See It *(cont.)*

See pages 43 and 44 for directions.

Innovator's Idea Sheet

You are an "Innovator." You have been given the task of inventing something new, unique, and usable. Your job is to "sell" your invention idea to those who have the ability to produce it. Your assignment is to convince others that your invention is innovative enough to be worthy of their attention.

Before you begin, consider the following information and suggestions to help you plan and execute your new idea.

What is an Invention?

An invention is something that happens as a result of someone trying to solve a problem or situation with which he or she is not content. Inventions are man-made and help make a person's life or job easier and/or quicker.

Consider the Television

Inventions affect history. Throughout history new ideas have often been dismissed as ridiculous, impractical, too radical, and so on. Imagine the conversations among people when they first heard about the new-fangled invention called television. Many people viewed this new invention with caution and concern. Before the twentieth century, people read books or listened to the radio and records to entertain themselves. What did they need a television for? Can you answer this question?

When you finally decide upon what to invent, consider how it will affect others and how you can convince them to consider the positive qualities of your invention.

Brainstorm

Brainstorming is an excellent way to get your thoughts organized and give your ideas a sense of direction. Brainstorm a list of man-made items that are common in a house, at school, or in the work place. Consider how each of these items helps people. Think of possible ways to improve upon or replace some of these items and list these as well.

Plan, Prepare, and Present

Choose one of your ideas to develop into an innovative product with the potential for acceptance by a large company. Prepare a list of materials you will need and make a plan for presenting the innovation to the class. Remember that you must convince your audience that this product will somehow improve their quality of life.

Use the "Innovators Planning Board" steps on page 48 to help you organize and carry out your invention idea. Think of your invention as a product that will solve a problem. Complete the Brainstorming Web provided by writing the invention in the center circle and listing in the boxes ways in which the invention will be useful in solving a problem.

Innovator's Planning Board

1. Think about a problem that needs solving.

2. Decide on a plan for an invention that will help solve the problem.

3. Illustrate or make a model of your invention.

4. Name your invention.

5. "Sell" your idea to a company (the class).

Reminder: The company to whom you will "sell" your invention receives thousands of new ideas each year claiming to enhance its products. You must convince them your invention is unique, practical, and feasible.

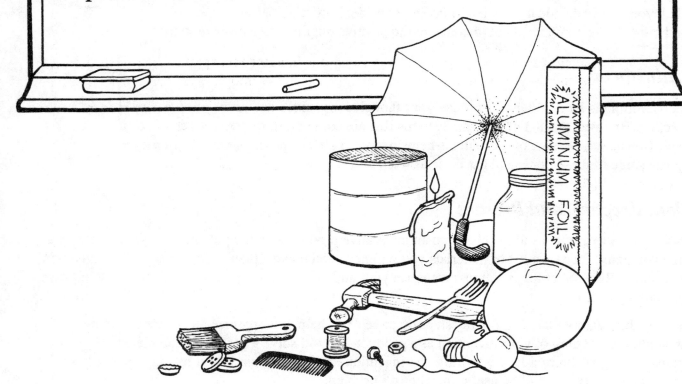

48

Inca Relay

Topic

The ancient Incas

Objective

Students will identify how the Inca Empire was bound together over the long distances which it encompassed. They will name at least one major engineering accomplishment of the Incas.

Materials

- a suitable outdoor area or gym
- a very simple message of the teacher's creation (See Procedure.)

Preparation

1. Create a message of approximately one or two sentences.
2. Procure space for activity and secure adequate time for use of space required.

Procedure

1. Space your students outside on the playground in a large circle about 100 feet (30 meters) apart. (If this is not feasible at an outdoor facility, divide your class into two groups, placing one group in one column or row about one hundred feet apart from the other group. Should inclement weather prevail, move the activity into the gym or large room with groups on either side of it.)

2. The teacher should start a message with one student from the circle (or from one row if you are using a two-group arrangement). The message should be no longer than one or two sentences. It does not necessarily have to be topical or curriculum-based in nature. A statement like, "The train to Columbus is leaving in two hours and will arrive after the ball game has begun," will suffice.

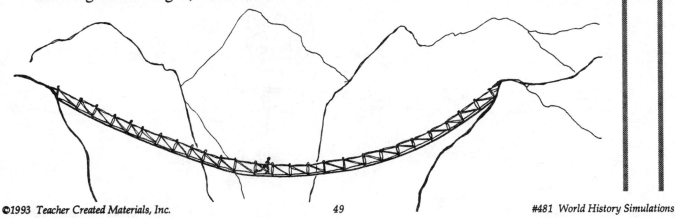

Inca Relay *(cont.)*

Procedure *(cont.)*

3. In turn, each student within the circle should orally relay the message to a peer in front of him or her. The last student transmits the message back to the teacher. (Those involved in the two single column relay groups should be sure to have each runner stand away from his/her group as the messenger arrives so the entire group cannot hear the message ahead of time.)

For Discussion

Students should be questioned as to why the Incas would base such a vital communications system on the relatively slow pace of humans.

Background

"Inca Relay" is intended to be a leg-stretching anticipatory set for undertaking studies of the Inca Empire of South America. The three thousand mile-long north to south empire was held together by an impressive system of roads, suspension bridges, and fleet runners to carry the ruler's orders. It was rather like a human "pony express," and a quite efficient one at that.

Follow-Up

Encourage students to research how far each runner had to travel and what climatic conditions they might have encountered.

Arrogant Mentor

Topic

The French Revolution

Objective

Students will name two causes of the French Revolution.

Materials

- a taste-tempting candy bar or pastry
- one cup of coffee or a soft drink
- the teacher's favorite book or magazine
- a class treat (optional)
- lunch or serving tray
- page 53, reproduced (one per student)

Preparation

1. Place all items on the tray out of students' view, but easily accessible to the teacher for use at the appropriate time.

2. Make copies of page 53 ahead of time so that students can give immediate feedback when necessary.

Procedure

1. On the day your class begins the French Revolution (but before that lesson is initiated) place the tray with its succulent pastry or other treat, a cup of coffee or a soft drink, and your choice of reading material next to you. (The class period right before lunch seems to be ideal.)

2. Depending upon the subject matter for that time of day, assign the class a lengthy review lesson or some other tedious task that will be sure to make the students grumble.

3. While they labor over the task, enjoy your tasty treat and relax with your reading material. Inconspicuously observe the students for any outward reactions that may surface due to your behavior. You may want to dramatize your actions further by commanding a student to retrieve some other object or treat for you from the lounge or office. Comments like, "I'd like to share, but you know how it is" are sure to arouse the ire of some students.

Arrogant Mentor *(cont.)*

Procedure *(cont.)*

4. As you introduce social studies and lead into the French Revolution, compare the insolent rule of Louis XVI to your own behavior. Make analogous the students' anger to that rage which flared in the hearts of the French peasants.

5. As a peace offering (if you feel so inclined), present a small edible treat to the class.

For Discussion

In many classrooms, students will be upset and complain about the teacher being so rude and callous as to relax with food and drink in front of those who are "putting their noses to the grindstone." As the anticipatory set for the French Revolution later that same day, provide students with copies of the questions on page 53. Ask them to express their feeling about your behavior earlier in the day. Discuss student responses. Have students keep their written reactions for a while so that they may compare their initial responses to those of the French populace during the French Revolution.

Background

In order to succeed at "Arrogant Mentor," you must feel extremely comfortable with your students. You will assume a role that most teachers are probably not accustomed to playing. (Then again, depending upon the circumstances of the particular day on which the lesson is presented, one might thoroughly enjoy the activity.)

If conducted successfully for the balance of *one* class period, this activity will speak volumes about the causes of the French Revolution. In the latter stages of "the divine right of kings," Louis XVI held on to an expensive court. The governmental institutions of the era kept the nobility well feathered at the expense of the masses through high taxation. The vast majority of the people were the overtaxed peasants while the aristocracy paid virtually no tax. This came at a time when the French national debt was extremely high and the people suffered from a poor wheat crop. The final vestiges of feudalism in France were soon to be violently cast away.

Follow-Up

Students may be encouraged to do a special project on the French Revolution. A diorama of the storming of the Bastille, a report on the causes and effects of the revolution, or a dramatized "newscast" where reporters deliver "live" accounts by means of a time machine are all interesting possibilities for students with different learning styles. Encourage your students to make suggestions.

Name _____

Arrogant Mentor Reaction Sheet

Directions: Write your responses to the following questions on the lines provided. Think about your reactions and feelings as you experienced the "Arrogant Mentor" simulation, as presented by your teacher.

How did you react to your teacher's behavior and manners while you had to work? _____

_____

_____

_____

_____

Was this situation fair or justified? How did it make you feel? _____

_____

_____

_____

_____

Did you gain or lose respect for your teacher? _____

_____

_____

_____

_____

How could your teacher have made the situation right with you? _____

_____

_____

_____

_____

Closed Society

Topic

Japan's two-and-one-half century self-imposed isolation (1600-1853)

Objective

Students will offer one reason for Japan's isolation from the rest of the world during its period of isolation. Student teams will try to decifer each other's "secret codes" based on terms relating to Japanese history, culture, and geography.

Materials

- page 56, reproduced (one copy per team)

- an acknowledgement for the success of winning team members (See page 94 for ideas.)

Preparation

1. Reproduce copies of page 56 in preparation for the team activity.

2. Prepare rewards.

Procedure

1. Divide the class into cooperative learning teams. Have each team use the text and other curriculum resource materials on Japanese history to select a secret three-word code. The code needs to contain three nouns — one dealing with Japanese history, one with Japanese geography, and one which refers to its economy. Provide a sample list of terms (page 56) to each group.

2. Each day allow every group to present three questions (one for each code word category) to the other teams. A team may direct its questions to one other team, or it may ask a different question to any three teams. All questions must be able to be answered with a simple "Yes" or "No."

3. In addition to the questions, students should depend upon notes from previous sessions in order to acquire necessary information to unlock the secret codes.

Closed Society *(cont.)*

Procedure (cont.)

4. The length of this activity is up to the teacher. It can last as long as groups of students are teamed together or for the duration of the unit of study on Japan.

5. The determined victor in "Closed Society" may also vary. The last team to have its code uncovered may be the designated winner as could the cooperative team that decoded the most hidden word systems. Whatever you choose as criteria to determine the winning team, you should consider honoring winners with some reward. Certificates, popcorn parties, reinforcer points, etc. are all possible incentives for students.

For Discussion

Direct the following questions to the teams at the close of the activity.

- What kept you (as a team) from divulging your secret to anyone else?
- Who kept Japan from opening itself to the outside world for 250 years? Why?

Background

Fear of foreign invasion and loss of feudal control of their homeland, Japanese shoguns kept their nation an island in the strictest sense of the word. From about 1600 to 1853 foreigners were not welcome in Japan, with the exception of a few European trading posts near Nagasaki. From missionaries to merchants, foreigners were deemed as potential schemers to overtake Nippon. Not until the power and might of the United States Navy under Commodore Matthew Perry steamed into Tokyo Bay did the warlords relent, and Japan began to catch up with the rest of the world at an alarming rate.

"Closed Society" does not begin to seclude students from each other. However, with an ample amount of teamwork and cooperation (virtues that are part of the foundation of Japanese tradition), they can maintain a secret code that others in the room will want to decipher. Verbal ingenuity, as well as careful listening and note-taking skills, can be used by teams come to guard information from others while protecting their own data.

Follow-Up

This activity need not be limited to what might be customarily considered social studies time. It can be used as a "sponge" activity in any subject anytime during the day when about ten minutes of "down time" is available.

Closed Society Code Words

See pages 54 and 55 for directions.

History	Geography	Culture
shogun	volcano	sumo
samurai	archipelago	baseball
emperor	island	Shintoism
Hiroshima	Honshu	sushi
Matthew Perry	Hokkaido	kimono
Hirohito	Mt. Fuji	judo
daimyo	Shikoku	Buddhism
Pearl Harbor	terrace	cooperation
missionaries	typhoons	shrines

Anything for a Buck

Topic

Foreign imperialism within China in the 1800's

Objective

Students will identify actions taken by Great Britain, America, and other foreign governments in securing trading privileges in China during the nineteenth century. Students will explain why nationalism grew in China during this time period.

Materials

- page 59, reproduced (one per student)

Preparation

1. Reproduce "Drug Lords of Medding" for cooperative team members.

Procedure

1. Divide the class into cooperative learning teams.

2. Distribute copies of the problem solving situation "Drug Lords of Medding" to each student.

3. Orally read the dilemma while the students silently peruse it.

4. Allow teams three to five minutes to discuss the possible actions they could undertake in the outlined situation.

5. Time permitting, individual teams could be paired up to share their ideas. At the very least, a whole class discussion should ensue where each team shares its viewpoints and responses to the dilemma.

6. Transfer the students' reaction to "Drug Lords of Medding" into the text lesson about coerced opium trade in China as a means of initiating foreign domination. Have them compare and contrast the simulated situation with that part of history known as the Opium War.

Anything for a Buck *(cont.)*

For Discussion

While most students will regard with disdain the gangs in "Drug Lords of Medding," it should be interesting to note their reactions to what amounted to "state sponsored" drug pushing within China by the British and other nations.

Ask the following questions to help students better understand China's position in the twentieth century as it turned inward and eventually embraced communism.

- Why would the Chinese workers buy the opium in the first place? How did such actions affect Chinese attitudes about foreigners?

- Who or what allowed such drug trade to go on?

Background

The Opium War of 1839-1842 enabled Great Britain to sell opium to Chinese workers and engage in huge profits. These moneys were subsequently used to buy Chinese tea. Shortly thereafter, other foreign powers, including the United States, forced self-serving trade concessions upon the Chinese. Weakened by corrupt and disorganized government, China was thoroughly exploited by the West and Japan for almost a century.

"Drug Lords of Medding" presents a very contemporary problem that some students may have had to deal with already. Although there are no easy answers to such a dilemma, students should realize the economic motive behind it.

Drug Lords of Medding

Medding is a large city of over one million people. Like any other city, it is made up of dozens of different neighborhoods. In the last several years a group of young thugs has veritably terrorized one poor neighborhood on the southeast side of the city.

This teenage gang, "The Outlaws," has been pushing marijuana, crack cocaine, and other drugs upon the youth of this neighborhood. They have made much money and have used it to buy cars, stereo equipment, and weapons. A few businesses, although aware that their money is tainted by drug deals, continue to sell goods to "The Outlaws" because they need the money to stay afloat.

In order to support their habit, many of the neighborhood youth have turned to crime to raise money. In the past three years alone, robberies and break-ins have increased fifty times the previous rate for these crimes.

To complicate matters further this trend of drug-peddling dangerous gangs has caught on in other neighborhoods. Medding is almost held captive by at least twenty known gangs within its city limits.

Questions to Consider

What do you think can be done to rid Medding of its problem?

Who, if anyone, do you think is at fault?

What people are in the best position to solve this problem?

"Dr. Livingston, I Presume"

Topic

Explorers of nineteenth century Africa

Objective

Students will identify three European explorers of Africa's interior and list three reasons for their expeditions. Students will follow directions and utilize measurement skills in deducing the solution to a problem.

Materials

- three copies of page 62
- three copies of page 63 (eight cards for each set)
- copies of page 64 for winning team (one per member)

Preparation

1. To prepare the "Lost in Africa" simulation, in which student teams locate three European explorers, label each of the three "Lost Explorer" illustrated copies (page 62) with a different name of a nineteenth century adventurer in Africa — Rene Caille, Heinrich Barth, or Dr. David Livingston.

2. Hide each of these illustrations in a very inconspicuous spot in your classroom (or school). Student teams will attempt to locate each "Lost Explorer," using specific clues.

3. Use copies of the "Lost in Africa" Clue Cards on page 63 to create eight sequential clues for each of the "Lost Explorer" illustrations you have just hidden. Use riddles to help students find the hidden location, or give step-by-step instructions involving measurement to integrate a math skill into the process. For example, if you have a large bookshelf or bookcase in your room, the clues could be ordered something like this:

   a. Stand on entrance door threshold.

   b. Walk in 126 inches (320 cm). Stop.

   c. Turn 90 degrees to your right.

   d. Proceed forward 3 yards and 2 feet (335 cm).

   e. Continue ahead 3 feet 8 inches (295 cm).

   f. Measure 50 inches (127 cm) up from the floor.

   g. Look in this book. (Be sure to have selected a little-used book.)

"Dr. Livingston, I Presume" (cont.)

Preparation (cont.)

4. Make copies of the reward on page 64 for the winning team members.

Procedure

1. Divide the class into cooperative learning teams.

2. After discussing Rene Caille, Heinrich Barth, and Dr. David Livingston in class, announce to the students that they will begin a search to locate the three missing explorers within the confines of the room (school). Any team that can locate pertinent information on any of these explorers will receive a peek at a clue.

3. Every time a team presents a different vital fact about the explorer's background, motivation, or discoveries, offer that group a glance at an ordered clue for the lost explorer of its choice. Do not relinquish clues to student teams. Give them an adequate amount of time to absorb the clue and no more. If they forget, they must present new information in order to see it again. (They may write it down.)

4. Each teacher needs to place appropriate time restrictions as to when such information can be forwarded to the teacher and students can search. For the most part, a free five-minute period is all that is required to forward new information.

5. To dissuade wild guesses around the room, stipulate that a team must offer specified information concerning its chosen explorer.

6. The first team to locate each of the "Lost Explorer" illustrations is deemed the winner.

Background

Until well into the 1800's Europeans knew as much about the interior of Africa as they did about the moon. Individuals such as Barth, Caille, and Livingston provided new revelations over a fifty-year period dealing with geography, flora and fauna, and the people who inhabited this vast region. Although these three were motivated primarily by adventure (Caille), a quest for knowledge (Barth and Livingston), and a desire to spread Christianity (Livingston), their information would eventually be employed by European governments in colonizing most of Africa.

Follow-Up

"Lost in Africa" could be interestingly altered by having student teams hide the "Lost Explorer" illustrations and write the clues necessary to find them.

Lost Explorer

_____
(Explorer's Name)

"Lost in Africa" Clue Cards

Lost in Africa

Clue:

Lost in Africa

Clue:

Lost in Africa

Clue:

Lost in Africa

Clue:

Lost in Africa

Clue:

Lost in Africa

Clue:

Lost in Africa

Clue:

Lost in Africa

Clue:

"Lost in Africa" Team Award

Congratulations

are in order for

_____
(Student's Name)

and his/her team.

Together you followed the clues and located the "Lost Explorers."

_____
(Teacher's Name)

Imperialist Review

Topic

Nineteenth and early twentieth century of Africa focusing on European colonial rule

Objective

Students will define imperialism. They will list at least two European nations that possessed colonies in Africa at one time and name two colonies each for those European nations, using names of present African nations. They will review pertinent information involving African history in preparation for a test or quiz.

Materials

- one 8 ounce (224 g) package of candy, such as M & M's®

- pages 67 and 68, reproduced on index paper or heavy stock

- teacher-created review questions of material relating to the history of Africa, especially the period of European colonial rule

- one small paper cup for each student

- six plastic spoons (or surgical latex gloves)

Preparation

1. Have ready the candy, paper cups, and spoons (or gloves).

2. Before class begins, make copies of the nation/colony cards (page 67 or 68). Cut out the thirty cards provided and give each student a card. Students will assume the identity of either a European nation or an African colony.

3. Have a source of possible review questions from your chapter or unit available.

Procedure

1. Distribute a paper cup containing five pieces of the candy to each student. Emphasize that they are not to handle the treat at this time.

2. Take the stack of nation/colony cards and randomly pass them out, one to a student. Be sure that all six of the European nation cards are distributed, with the rest of the cards being from the African colony group.

Imperialist Review *(cont.)*

Procedure *(cont.)*

3. Have the students take their cups of candy and arrange themselves into six teams which are formed according to the European nation cards they hold. A team is formed by having all nation card holders whose nations or colonies are linked come together as a group. (For example, card holders of Libya, Somalia, and Italy would be a team.) **Some teams, such as the British and French contingents, will be significantly larger than others.**

4. Give the card holder of each European nation card a plastic spoon or surgical glove. (Handle candy in this fashion throughout the game.)

5. For this activity, when a student answers a review question correctly, that student (nation or colony) will have another piece of candy added to his/her cup. At the end of the competition, each holder of a European nation card will secure one piece more than half of each of his colonies' holdings of candy. For example, if a colony had four pieces of candy, the European nation would take three pieces; if a colony had six pieces, Europe would take four pieces, etc. Make sure students are apprised of this reward system in advance.

6. Proceed with the review game. Ask questions calling upon the student who first raises his/her hand for the answer. If a student is incorrect, call upon a second player, if possible. If not, drop that question and go onto another, eventually returning to the previous question. End after a specified time limit or question limit is reached.

For Discussion

At the end of the game, discuss the feelings of the students who represented colonies, using the following questions:

- How did it make you feel when you saw your knowledge (resources) benefit another player (nation)?

- Did some of you not play as well as you might have played for yourself?

- As a European "mother country," did you feel it was important for your "colonies" to do well? Why?

Background

Africa was carved into sections by European nations by the second half of the nineteenth century. Africans had little say in what was happening. They furnished labor for their imperialist European masters and endured severely limited political rights and freedoms.

In ''Imperialist Review,'' all but six of the students will be forced by the rules of the game to be in servitude to their ''colonial masters'' in order to win items (candy) for the masters, knowing that most of their resources will be turned over to their '' mother country.''

European Nation/African Colony Cards

Cut out the cards. See pages 65 and 66 for directions.

Italy	**Belgium**	**Libya** ◆ ◆ ◆ **Italy**
Angola ◆ ◆ ◆ **Portugal**	**Namibia** ◆ ◆ ◆ **Germany**	**Nigeria** ◆ ◆ ◆ **Great Britain**
South Africa ◆ ◆ ◆ **Great Britain**	**Algeria** ◆ ◆ ◆ **France**	**Madagascar** ◆ ◆ ◆ **France**
Mauritania ◆ ◆ ◆ **France**	**Great Britain**	**France**
Somalia ◆ ◆ ◆ **Italy**	**Mozambique** ◆ ◆ ◆ **Portugal**	**Ghana** ◆ ◆ ◆ **Great Britain**

European Nation/African
Colony Cards *(cont.)*

Cut out the cards. See pages 65 and 66 for directions.

Kenya ◆ ◆ ◆ **Great Britain**	**Zimbabwe** ◆ ◆ ◆ **Great Britain**	**Senegal** ◆ ◆ ◆ **France**
Mali ◆ ◆ ◆ **France**	**Ivory Coast** ◆ ◆ ◆ **France**	**Portugal**
Zaire ◆ ◆ ◆ **Belgium**	**Tanzania** ◆ ◆ ◆ **Germany**	**Uganda** ◆ ◆ ◆ **Great Britain**
Egypt ◆ ◆ ◆ **Great Britain**	**Sudan** ◆ ◆ ◆ **Great Britain**	**Morocco** ◆ ◆ ◆ **France**
Tunisia ◆ ◆ ◆ **France**	**Chad** ◆ ◆ ◆ **France**	

Entangling Alliances

Topic

World War I

Objective

Students will offer one cause of World War I.

Materials

• page 71, reproduced for each student

Preparation

Make copies of the "Entangling Alliances Dilemma".

Procedure

1. Divide the class into cooperative learning groups. Four persons per group would be the optimum for this activity. Each team should select a team reporter or spokesperson to later share with the class.

2. Distribute the dilemma to each student and orally read it while students read it silently.

3. Allow the students about three to five minutes to discuss the scenario within their teams. Discussion within each group should initially be done in pairs followed by having both pairs of students sharing their ideas with each other. This allows every student ample opportunity to express their predictions.

4. Teams should try to reach consensus on what will happen, but total agreement is not mandatory.

5. Team reporters should share with the class what the basic opinion of their group was concerning the outcome of this situation. While not necessarily the only viable prediction, the possibility of serious trouble between the two groups of boys involving the use of weapons is one that will crop up with many teams.

Entangling Alliances *(cont.)*

For Discussion

After all groups have shared their thoughts, ask the following questions:

- What alienated the groups of boys in the first place?

- What caused the build up in weapons?

- What would be the consequences of such a fight?

- How could such a confrontation be avoided?

- At what point in this situation would an open, honest airing of grievances between the groups of boys really have benefitted them?

Students will get into this discussion because it closely simulates life within certain social strata (perhaps including their own), although the use of weapons may or may not be part of their particular environment.

Read and cover the introductory material on World War I from your text. Afterward, compare the situation from the simulation to that at the beginning of "The War to End All Wars." Small problems escalated, bigger and bigger weapons were produced, and intense nationalism (or pride) kept sides from communicating.

Background

Entangling Alliances is an anticipatory set for the study of World War I. Nations, owing to the fact that they are run by humans, often take on negative and positive characteristics of the human condition. At the dawn of the twentieth century, the old line powers of Great Britain, France, and Russia (the Triple Entente) beheld the newly-formed militaristic state of Germany with leery eyes. Austria- Hungary (which was allied with Germany) viewed Kaiser Wilhelm II as the power to keep its crumbling empire together.

European nations began a steady growth in war material in preparation for a seemingly inevitable conflict. Serbia, relatively insignificant as a world power, had been nonetheless coveted by Austria- Hungary. The assassination of Archduke Ferdinand was the spark to set the fire that would fuse two separate alliances against each other and, in a domino effect, engulf an entire world in war.

Entangling Alliances Dilemma *(cont.)*

Dave, a strong, athletic fourteen-year-old, is in his second year at Smithfield Junior High. Ever since he moved into the district last year, his physical abilities on the football field and his daring and sometimes rude personality have rubbed many other students the wrong way. He has steadily alienated himself from teammates, Brian and Bob, with his aggressive style both on and off the field. Other students who are not athletes, Bill and Ben, have also had problems with Dave in the cafeteria and the halls. Ben, Bill, Brian, and Bob, rarely seen together before eighth grade, have started hanging out together, using their growing dislike of Dave as their common bond. Dave's macho character has attracted some followers who are pleased to share in Dave's status as a "dude not to mess with." Doug and Dwight are the two guys most often seen in the company of Dave. These two, who wouldn't make any class member's popularity list, revel in the attention they get from being part of "Dave's group."

As football seasons ends, Brian's and Bob's disdain of Dave is at an all-time high when Brian discovers Dave has a billy-club device in his football locker. Braced for future trouble, each begins packing brass knuckles. Meanwhile, Dwight has heard about the brass knuckles being carried by Brian and Bob, and he has informed Dave. Dave starts carrying a switchblade knife strapped to his ankle under his pant leg. One afternoon on the way home from school, Ben and Dwight (who have hated each other since a cafeteria incident in fifth grade) get into a shouting match during which Dwight lets it "slip" that Dave is armed with a knife, and that Ben better lay off. Shortly afterward, Ben lets Brian, Bob, and Bill know about the knife that Dave is concealing. Bill, a very loyal and faithful follower, secretly decides to begin toting a hidden handgun.

The very next day at recess, Dwight is hit by a rock on the playground by an unknown assailant. Dwight swears to the principal that it had to be Ben, but no proof is offered to implicate Ben. Dave tells Dwight later that afternoon not to worry, everything is going to be set right. Dave tells Dwight to follow him after school.

Questions to Consider

What do you predict is going to happen next? Why?

Masters of the World

Topic

The rise of Adolf Hitler in 1930's Germany

Objective

Students will define "demagogue." They will offer one way that Hitler was able to gain control of the German people.

Materials

- The following activity presents a powerful simulation designed to demonstrate the circumstances surrounding the rise to power of Adolf Hitler. Its success depends upon the cooperative involvement of the school administrator and the care and sensitivity in which the simulation is executed.

Preparation

1. Discuss the activity and the principal's involvement with him or her.

Procedure

1. Choose a group of students that have a common bond of some sort of excellence (e.g., safety patrol, top reading group or math group, science fair team) to be arbitrarily selected by the principal to be recipients of some special favors. The group should not have a closed membership. In other words, entrance into it could still be possible based on some student initiated behavior such as improved scores or advancing to a higher reading group. Do not choose student groups based on physical, ethnic, or racial characteristics. Somewhere in their school career, students may have already been exposed to a similar simulation utilizing hair or eye color. Racial and ethnic considerations are, needless to say, too sensitive and volatile to be implemented and should not be employed.

2. Arrange with your principal to come into your room early in the day to make a special pronouncement. His/her announcement should extol the virtues of the specific group selected (e.g., "In light of the science fair team's commitment to their projects and their outstanding performance...," "Since the safety patrol is out in all kinds of weather safe-guarding the younger students...," etc.).

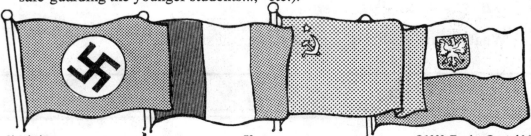

Masters of the World *(cont.)*

Procedure (cont.)

3. This edict should conclude with the principal outlining special privileges in effect from this point onward throughout the year for the select group. These privileges may include being first in the cafeteria line, a reduction of homework assignments, automatic "bonus" grades on a weekly basis, special Friday movie presentations, whatever you believe will be perceived as a valuable perk in the eyes of the general student population.

4. You will want to note the reactions of the "elite" to their surprising good fortune. How they respond to it (and subsequently to their non-privileged classmates) should be examined in a closing discussion.

5. Equally important, will be close examination of the reactions from the remainder of the students. The principal's announcement will make a powerful impact on the class. Again, follow-up discussion should definitely include the perceptions of the less-than-privileged.

   Note to the teacher: Whatever the group chosen, whatever the privileges granted, do not allow this simulation to live out that particular day. Powerful, negative emotions may build up if the activity is not defused and processed the same day. Undoubtedly, parents would have quite a number of legitimate questions that evening if the students were not properly debriefed. It is best for "Masters of the World" to be limited to half a day. Arrangements should then be made to meet with the class in order to debunk the principal's announcement and discuss its relevance to their learning. This activity is not prescribed for every class. Each instructor should properly gauge the ability of his/her students to handle the activity.

For Discussion

Make it very clear that the principal's orders were nothing but a deception. However, before the rationale is released to the students, elicit from them emotions they held. Initiate discussion by asking the "chosen ones" the following questions:

- What did it feel like to be elevated in status and given such perks?

- Did your mood change during the course of the day?

- What were your feelings toward the principal?

- Had this gone on for a period of days or weeks, how might you have changed?

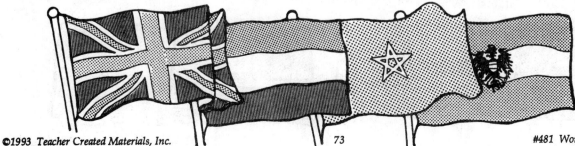

Masters of the World *(cont.)*

For Discussion *(cont.)*

Ask the rest of the class the following questions:

- How did it feel to be excluded from this group?
- Did you feel powerless, or did you believe that you, too, could join this group sometime later?
- Had it gone on for days or weeks, how might you have dealt with it?
- What were your feelings toward the principal?

After this emotional debriefing, introduce the topic of demagoguery and how a demagogue stirs up people's emotions. Discuss how such a leader will try to develop a false sense of pride in a group of people based on prejudices in order to gain power for him/herself. Discuss how Adolf Hitler was able to do the same with the masses in Germany in the early 1930's building up the ego of the German people at the expense of non-Germans, especially the Jewish population.

Background

Hitler was able to rule an entire intelligent nation through the use of grandiose promises, intimidation, and the creation of a superiority complex with his idea of Aryan dominance. Many Germans, downtrodden after World War I, eagerly bought Hitler's "Super Race" contention that promoted the image of the blue-eyed, blond-haired German as the epitome of God's intention for mankind. The most elite of this group (members of the Nazis, particularly the Gestapo) benefitted enormously in rank and privilege within the German social and political structure.

During the simulation the students were faced with a situation in which certain members of the class, due to authoritarian-prescribed characteristics were the pick of the class. They were held before their peers as models to be emulated.

Follow-Up

While Masters of the World is an anticipatory set designed to begin an investigation into some of the causes of World War II, after the unit has been completed you may want to refer to it for these thought-provoking questions:

- Could what happened in Germany in the 1930's under Hitler ever happen in the United States? Why or why not?

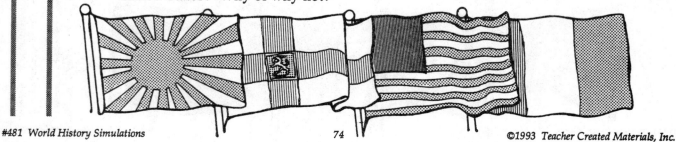

Gandhi

Topic

Mohandas K. Gandhi

Objective

Students will identify nonviolent civil disobedience as Gandhi's way of achieving
independence for India from Great Britain.

Materials

page 77, reproduced for each student

Preparation

Make copies of the dilemma facing the village of Mok.

Procedure

1. Divide the class into cooperative learning teams.

2. As an anticipatory set leading into a lesson about Gandhi and India's independence
   from Great Britain, distribute the copies of "In the Village of Mok" to each student.

3. Orally read the dilemma as students peruse it silently.

4. Give the teams about three to five minutes to discuss possible action that they would
   take in this situation.

Gandhi *(cont.)*

For Discussion

Allow teams to share their responses with one other team. Survey each team during a follow-up class discussion as to what they would do under such trying circumstances as those that face the villagers of Mok.

Introduce Gandhi and his methods (e.g., peaceful protest, sit-down strikes, boycotts) and compare them to the ideas the students may have developed. Proceed with the next lesson.

Background

A truly amazing man, Mohandas K. Gandhi rallied India's masses by cultivating nonviolent protest against further British rule in his country. Although Gandhi believed in nonviolence, he believed that violence was better than cowardice. Mohandas Gandhi, called Mahatma (Great Soul) by his followers, practiced a method of achieving social action through courage, truth, and nonviolence. This method, called satyagraha, was based on the idea that what you believe supercedes what you achieve. Satyagraha provided the foundation for India's independence and social change. Gandhi's innovative use of civil disobedience is thought to have been one motivating factor for Martin Luther King Jr.'s use of the same technique in the American civil rights movement.

Follow-Up

If you have a video camera at your disposal, you might encourage students to dramatize one instance where Gandhi put civil disobedience to work. Student research will have to precede the dramatization.

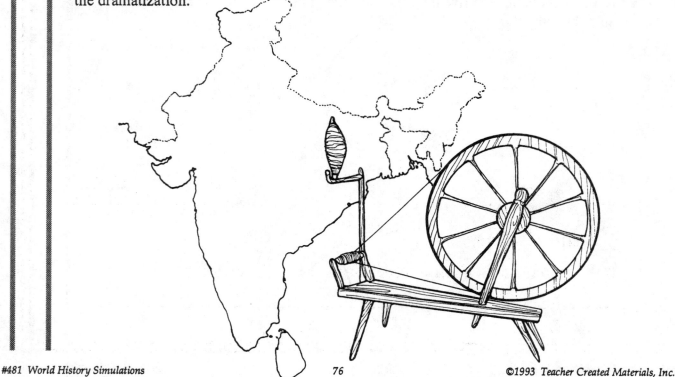

In the Village of "Mok"

You are the mayor of the village of Mok in the land of Aidni. Your country is ruled by the foreign nation of Trib which is thousands of miles away. However, its soldiers have been stationed in Aidni for over one hundred years. The people greatly resent the presence of the soldiers on their soil.

In the past year many members of your own village have been actively involved in trying to get the army of Trib out of Aidni. In the last week soldiers of Trib have killed and beaten several innocent villagers while investigating acts of sabotage against their supply depot which is close to Mok. While your people did in fact destroy supplies of the Trib army in the past, they have never before injured any soldier of Trib.

You have called the leading citizens of Mok together to confer about what you will do.

Question to Consider

What course of action will you suggest for the village of Mok?

Mao vs. Chiang

Topic

Twentieth century history of China

Objective

Students will denote advantages and disadvantages each side had in the communist/nationalist Chinese civil war. Students will answer pertinent chapter review questions in preparation for a quiz or test.

Materials

- teacher-created (or text) review questions about modern China
- pages 80 and 81, reproduced for each team

Preparation

1. Create your own review questions or use ready-made questions pertaining to the topic.
2. Copy pages 80 and 81 onto index paper or heavy stock.

Procedure

1. Divide the class into two heterogeneous teams. Be sure neither side is top heavy with advanced students.

2. Explain to the class that in review for the upcoming test on twentieth century China they will participate in a review game known as "Mao vs. Chiang." Randomly choose which sides will represent Mao and Chiang.

3. Each team will receive a set of six questions to which they will respond in alternate turns with the opposing team.

4. Ask the first team a review question. A response of any sort (correct or incorrect) is followed by the teacher drawing a consequence card for either the Communist (Mao) or Nationalist (Chiang) team, depending upon which team is answering.

5. For a correct response, the teacher selects a positive consequence card. An incorrect answer dictates the selection of a negative consequence card.

Mao vs. Chiang *(cont.)*

Procedures (cont.)

6. When a team has used all of its positive consequence cards, it can no longer score points until it has gone through its six question rotation. If a correct answer is offered after all positive cards have been used, no points are added or taken away. At any time, an incorrect answer may result in points deducted dependent upon the negative consequence card drawn.

7. Alternate questions between teams.

8. Since their are only two teams, team responses may be selected in a variety of manners.

    a. Each student on a team answers in turn.

    b. The team member with his/her hand raised first responds.

    c. The student with the first raised hand on a team responds with no one allowed to answer two questions in a row.

    d. Time limited team conference responses are permitted. Allow thirty seconds or so for team members to confer on an answer.

9. The game concludes when the six-question limit has been reached. The team having the most points wins. If time permits, a second rotation of another six questions may be added.

Background

The Chinese civil war, which was over twenty years long and culminated after World War II, pitted two cunning (and often ruthless) leaders against each other. Mao Tse-Tung (Zedong) led the communist forces which drew enormous popular support from the hundreds of millions of downtrodden peasants. Chiang Kai-shek headed the nationalist army that had the blessing of Western governments and the wealthy segment of Chinese society.

Through the consequence cards, the significant differences in the foundation of each of these two armies are emphasized. The array of negative cards, especially on the nationalist side, makes evident the eventual victor in this struggle, even though it is possible for Chiang's team to win the review activity.

Mao vs. Chiang Consequence Cards

Reproduce and cut out consequence cards. See pages 78 and 79 for directions.

Consequence Card Key:

NCPC = Nationalist (Chiang) Positive Consequences

NCNC = Nationalist (Chiang) Negative Consequences

CMPC = Communist (Mao) Positive Consequences

CMNC = Communist (Mao) Negative Consequences

NCPC

Chiang's army is very well equipped.

(+10 points)

NCPC

Chiang's Nationalist army is financially supported by foreign powers.

(+10 points)

NCNC

Chiang's army shows little concern towards the poor peasants.

(-5 points)

NCNC

Corrupt government officials grow rich on the Nationalist side.

(-5 points)

NCNC

Chiang's Nationalist army loses support of the peasants.

(-5 points)

Mao vs. Chiang Consequence Cards *(cont.)*

Reproduce and cut out consequence cards. See pages 78 and 79 for directions.

NCNC

Chiang's Nationalist army flees to Taiwan in 1949.

(-10 points)

CMPC

Peasants supply Mao's forces with food and goods.

(+5 points)

CMPC

Mao opposes foreign involvement in China.

(+5 points)

CMPC

Communist army help peasants plant and harvest crops.

(+5 points)

CMPC

Mao's Communists share land with peasants.

(+5 points)

CMPC

Mao's Communists take over mainland China in 1949.

(+10 points)

CMNC

Mao's forces are very poorly equipped.

(-5 points)

CMNC

Foreign nations such as the United States supply Chiang in order to defeat Mao.

(-5 points)

A "Red" White Elephant Sale

Topic

A basic overview of communism

Objective

Students will learn that in communism there is no private ownership of business enterprises. They will identify the state as the sole proprietor of business and strict regulator of what and how much should be produced.

Materials

- selected "white elephant" items that students are responsible for bringing in for their sale

- page 84, reproduced

Preparation

1. Reproduce and cut out enough copies of "Red Star" money on page 84. Allocate about one hundred dollars for each student.

2. Several days before introducing a lesson on the philosophy and workings of communism, divide the class into cooperative learning teams.

3. Explain to the class that you would like them to conduct a "white elephant" sale of items they possess that they believe other students in the class (or other classes) would like to have. It is to be part of a math lesson on money.

4. Tell students that you will extend reinforcer points to each team depending on how much they sell. For instance, you could say that for every ten dollars they sell to students outside of their own team, you will add one bonus point to their ongoing reinforcement schedule. Furthermore, explain that on sale day you will make some "minor" restrictions which will be dealt with at that time. (If you do not have a reinforcement point schedule in effect, you may introduce one or create a list of ranked special privileges as an incentive for greater sales.)

5. Teams are to brainstorm items their "store" could sell, such as trading cards, old toys, or home-made snacks. Make sure students realize that they may only sell their own personal items, not those belonging to their siblings or others. You may wish to prepare a letter, similar to the "Information/Request Letter" on page 29, explaining the need for the items and purpose of the activity to parents.

6. In advance of the sale, student teams should make advertisement signs, easily visible price lists, and any other provisions necessary for a successful sale.

A "Red" White Elephant Sale *(cont.)*

Procedure

1. On the sale day, distribute one hundred dollars in "Red Star" bills to each student participating in the sale.

2. After the money has been passed out, go around to each team and inform them of the following: you will be limiting the items they can sell by disallowing a sizable portion of the selection of goods that they had made available; all money is to be directly handed over to you after each sale. (You may want student teams to keep track of their own accounts before they turn the money over to you. The emphasis here is on a higher authority regulating markets and stifling profit incentive.)

3. After the sale has continued in this over-regulated fashion for ten minutes or so, return all moneys to the rightful teams and eliminate the goods restrictions so that a successful sale may occur.

For Discussion

As an anticipatory set for a follow-up lesson on communism ask students what they were feeling when the restrictions of the sale were imposed and profits were confiscated. Introduce the basic tenets of communism (i.e., no private ownership of business, total governmental control of business, no capitalistic profit incentive) by asking students if the restrictions took the fun out of the sale. If so, in what way?

Background

As communism begins to fade out of the world scene, it is still important to look at what made it appear workable and at the same time spelled out its demise. Having everyone totally equal (at least in theory, though definitely not in practice) in an economic sense was its goal. In order to accomplish that, it thwarted inner human urges to better one's self and prosper. With motivation squelched, apathy set in. Production was ineptly controlled by the state's dogmatic rule, and goods were hard to keep in supply.

Even in a nation that had never known more than a modest standard of living like the former Soviet Union, as modern communications technology made the Soviet citizenry aware of what was out in the rest of world, they demanded much more than communist ideologies could produce. A "Red" White Elephant Sale gives students a small dose of how a command economy under communist rule would have operated.

"Red Star" Money

The Republic of Red Star

$5

The Republic of Red Star

$20

The Republic of Red Star

$1

The Republic of Red Star

$10

Cold War

Topic

The "Cold War" between the United States and the Soviet Union (1946-1991)

Objective

Students will offer one reason for the tension between the United States and the Soviet Union in the post World War II era.

Materials

- pages 87 and 88, reproduced for each student
- page 89, reproduced for each cooperative learning team

Preparation

1. Make copies of the "Smith vs. Allen" dilemma.
2. Prepare copies of the reaction sheet on page 89.

Procedure

1. Before initiating a lesson on the post World War II relationship between the United States and the Soviet Union, divide the class into cooperative learning teams. Each group should select a spokesperson.

2. Pass out copies of "Smith vs. Allen" to each member of the class.

3. Read the simulation aloud to the class and have each group discuss possible ramifications of the situation within its team. Distribute one copy of the reaction sheet on page 89 to each team. Allow time for each team to write its reaction to the dilemma. (If time permits, teams may pair up with each other for further discussion before class interaction.)

4. Have the spokesperson from each learning team present his/her group's interpretation of the causes and probable consequences of the dilemma, using the team's reaction sheet responses.

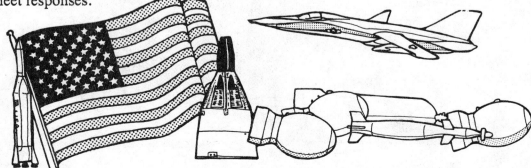

Cold War *(cont.)*

For Discussion

After all reporters or spokespersons have shared, open the floor to the entire class. If the dilemma's stated questions have been sufficiently covered in previous discussion, focus on what courses of action could be taken by either side to effect a peaceful solution.

Pose the following questions:

* Do you think it is possible to effect a peaceful solution? If so, how?

The idea that no direct communication has occurred between the two families should be discussed at this time. If either side feels even more threatened, upon what other protective devices can they rely?

Background

The "Smith vs. Allen" simulation attempts to approximate the global confrontation between two superpowers (U.S.A. vs. U.S.S.R.) that endured for forty-five years primarily on the emotions of fear and mistrust. The Soviet Union (Russia) had a centuries-old record of being invaded. To this fact add two significant events of World War II. First, Nazi Germany's reneging on a non-aggression pact and its subsequent invasion thrust Stalinist Russia into a war in which twenty million of its people would die. Coupled with that horrifying reality was America's unleashing of an atomic weapon upon Japan. The Soviet Union scrambled to match American technology.

The United States, on the other hand, seemed to be caught totally off guard by the Japanese attack on Pearl Harbor. It was determined never to be surprised again, and it put its massive economic and military resources to work in order to secure that goal.

The two powers therefore set out on a course that would see each try to out do the other's military might in hopes of obtaining national peace of mind. The Soviet economy, however, could not withstand the strain imposed upon it by the decades-long military race and so collapsed by 1991. With it came the downfall of the arms race and the Cold War.

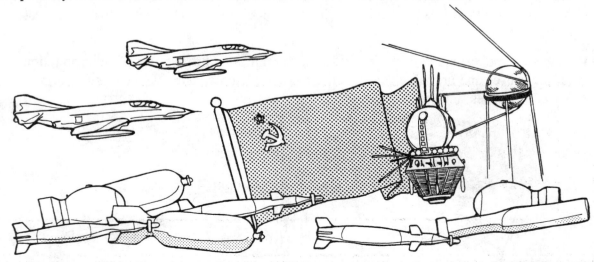

"Smith vs. Allen"

Look at the diagram on page 88. This diagram shows the location of two families that have had recent tragedies. The Smith family, who resides on Hill S, has eight members. However, just last year four other members of this family were murdered by an intruder, a person the family knew and had apparently trusted. The Allen family lives on Hill A. The Allen family has four members. There had been five in the family when one of the Allens was ambushed along a fence row on the far corner of their property a half mile from their house.

The murderers in both cases were caught and punished by the legal system. They no longer pose a threat to these families. In no way was either family responsible for the other family's grief. Lately however, Mr. Allen has been taking a lot of target practice with several new high-powered rifles he purchased. Some of these weapons are equipped with long-range telescopic sights. (He hopes to better secure his family and property.)

The Smiths often hear shooting going on across the valley and are very disturbed by it. Mr. Smith has put a high fence around his property and has bought several weapons of his own in the past few months.

Questions to Consider

What do you think might happen in this situation?

Why do you think the situation has progressed to the point that it has?

"Smith vs. Allen" Diagram

See pages 85 to 87 for directions.

The Smiths

The Allens

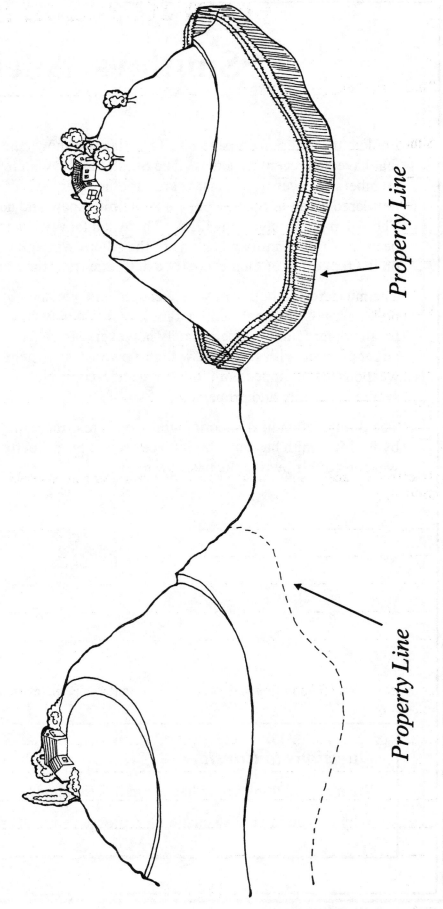

Property Line

Property Line

Team Reaction Sheet

Team Members_____

Situation: _____

_____

_____

_____

_____

We see the problem as follows: _____

_____

_____

_____

_____

To effect a peaceful solution, the course of action that can be taken by Smith family could be the following:

_____

_____

_____

_____

_____

To effect a peaceful solution, the course of action that can be taken by Allen family could be the following:

_____

_____

_____

_____

_____

The "Mole People"

Topic

South African apartheid

Objective

Students will define apartheid and identify where it has been official policy, who has been separated from whom, and what is presently being done about it.

Materials

- page 92, reproduced (one copy for each student)

Preparation

1. Make copies of the situation titled "Mole People at Midfield."

Procedure

1. Divide the class into cooperative learning teams. Each team should have a team spokesperson or reporter.

2. Pass out the situation, "Mole People at Midfield," to each student and orally read it while having them silently read through it.

3. Have teams confer for several minutes to decide on how they would respond in that predicament.

4. Have team reporters share with the class each group's ideas about handling the dilemma presented in the simulation.

The "Mole People" *(cont.)*

For Discussion

Ask the class about what they view as the apparent injustices of this situation. Use this as a springboard for a discussion about apartheid.

Background

As of 1992, apartheid had been officially practiced in the Union of South Africa for over forty years, but it was in its initial stages of dismantling. Social pressure from within and economic pressure from without the nation had led President F.W. DeKlerk to seek a referendum from the white governing population to begin to repeal the various codes of "apartness." By nearly a two-to-one margin, white voters agreed to do away with it. However, the white minority on this issue promised to keep opposing the destruction of apartheid. Much of their fear of losing apartheid is an economic one, a fear they will lose land that has been in their families for generations.

Follow-Up

Have students (as teams or individuals) research apartheid.

Encourage students to bring in and share articles from newspapers and news magazines as the issue of apartheid continues to surface in current events on almost a weekly basis. Create a bulletin board or "On-Going Issue" center in which to keep researched information and articles for the class to read, discuss, and assess. Provide time during the day or week for groups to meet in order to come to decisions and air opinions on the issue. Come together for class discussion after groups have had an opportunity to consider the question and problems associated with apartheid.

"Mole People at Midfield"

You are in your second year at Midfield Middle School. You moved to Midfield when your father finally got a job there after being laid off from his last job for six months. He claims this is the best job he has ever had. Last year you wondered about certain happenings in the school but were either too young or too indifferent to care about them. However, this year you are beginning to notice this disturbing pattern of events occurring all over again as school takes off in September.

Here are some of the things you have experienced:

Your classes usually have about twenty-five students in them. Yet, on occasion you have seen one class that consistently has forty-five students in it. In fact, this same grouping of pupils is together all the time. They never separate, no matter what the subject.

In a school this large (1,123 students) it could be possible to not notice this one group of students. However, once again you have seen them come to eat in the cafeteria after everyone else was done. They were eating the scraps left behind.

You have started playing on the school soccer team this year, and you have friends on the football team. Neither you nor your friends have seen any of the members from this one group on any team, even though some looked as if they could be rather athletic.

What piqued your curiosity was viewing the group of forty-five students leave on the same bus one afternoon well after the other buses had left, at least a half hour later. You decided to question the principal, Mr. Harsh.

Mr. Harsh pulls no punches; he tells it like he sees it. "You're new to Midfield aren't you? Well, listen well, listen once, and ask no more. Those forty-five people are different. Each and every last one has a birth mark somewhere on their body. How do I know? Well, in Midfield we make it our business to know right from the time they're delivered at Midfield Hospital. Everyone knows they're not like everybody else. We're supposed to educate them, to a certain degree. But we won't have them mingle much with the rest of our students. We call them "Mole People." They all live in the same rundown part of town on the east end by the mines. Their ancestors used to own the mines. In fact, that's all they'll do when they leave school, dig in those mines. It's best you just ignore them and go on about your business. You're dismissed. Oh, by the way, you wouldn't have a birthmark by any chance?"

Questions to Consider

Does this situation bother you? Why? If it does, to whom will you protest? What will you do? Why?

Simulation Savvy Certificate

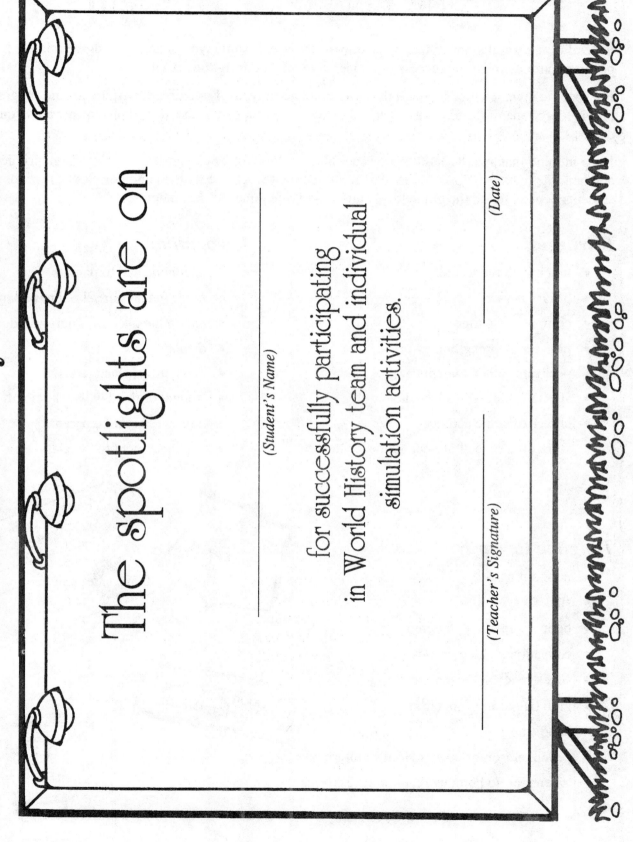

The spotlights are on

_____
(Student's Name)

for successfully participating
in World History team and individual
simulation activities.

_____
(Teacher's Signature)

_____
(Date)

Awards and Rewards

Several of the simulations in this book suggest the use of some type of acknowledgment in the form of a positive reinforcement for success or cooperative effort during the activities.

If a specific reward is not stated in the simulation activity, or if you do not wish to use the suggestions provided, try one of the alternatives listed below. This is a partial list of the kinds of rewards you might decide to use.

Keep in mind that awards and rewards can fall into three major categories — recognition, privileges, and tangible rewards. No single kind of reinforcement works better than another. Select rewards for students depending on the grade level and/or the preferences of the students.

Privileges

- lunch with the teacher
- library pass
- computer use time
- pass for skipping homework
- peer tutor other students
- special "helper" for the day
- choice of some activity
- work on a special project, game, center, etc.

Recognition

- telephone call to parents
- name in class or school newspaper
- pat on the back for a job well done
- display work
- class cheer, chant, etc.
- student of the day, week, month
- note sent home to parents
- announcement to the class

Tangible Rewards

- popcorn party
- stickers
- bonus points or extra credit
- educational video or movie
- snack treats in the classroom
- grab bag or treasure chest
- hand stamp
- pencil, eraser, or other school supply
- tokens for no homework, extra recess, etc.

You may wish to use the map below as part of the extension tools for related cooperative team activities and simulations. Distribute copies to students as needed. Or prepare a transparency for use on the overhead projector.

World Map

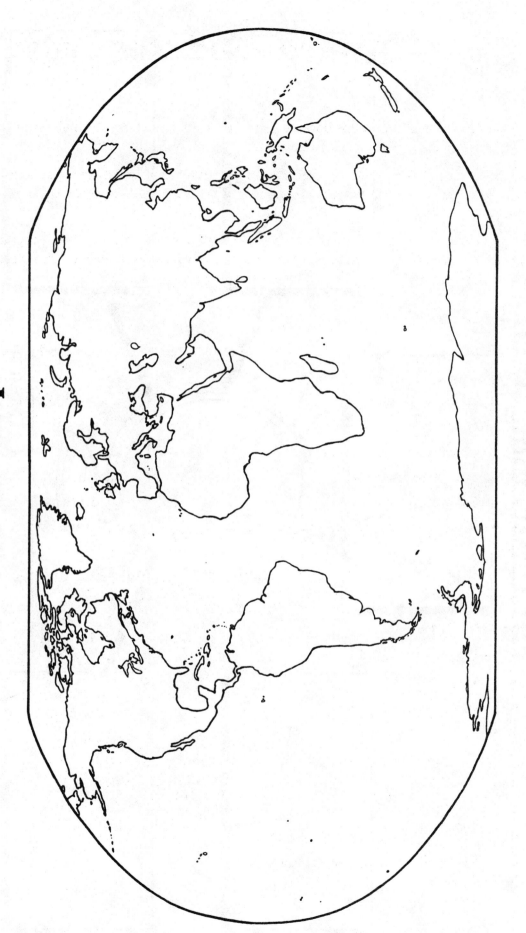

Brainstorming Web

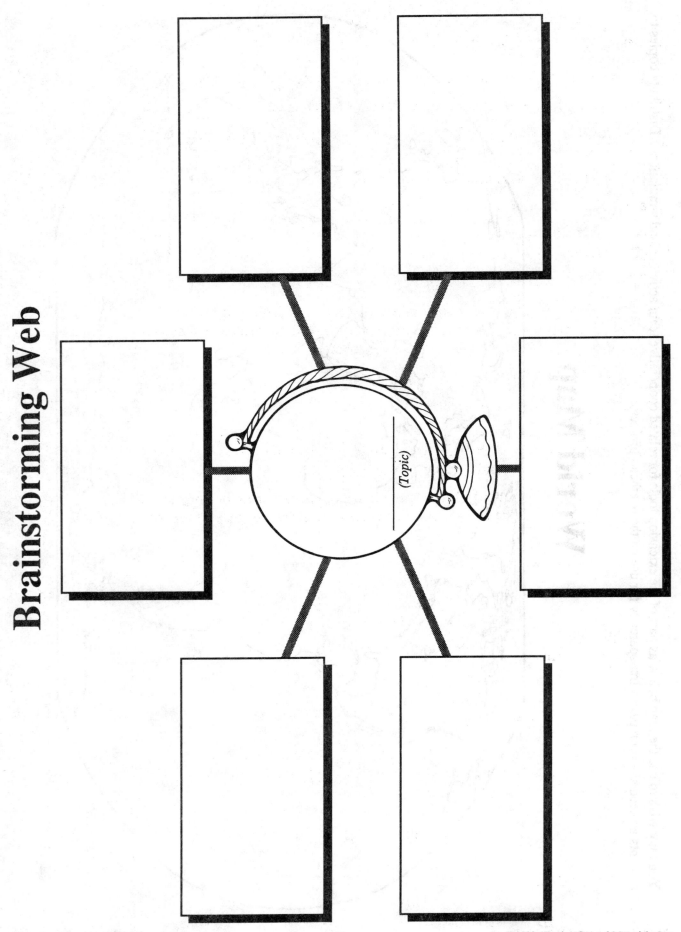

(Topic)